Midwifing—A Womanist Approach to Pastoral Counseling

Midwifing—A Womanist Approach to Pastoral Counseling

Investigating the Fractured Self, Slavery, Violence, and the Black Woman

Myrna Thurmond-Malone

FOREWORD BY
Pamela Ayo Yetunde

☙PICKWICK *Publications* • Eugene, Oregon

MIDWIFING—A WOMANIST APPROACH TO PASTORAL COUNSELING
Investigating the Fractured Self, Slavery, Violence, and the Black Woman

Copyright © 2019 Myrna Thurmond-Malone. All rights reserved. Except for brief quotations in critical publications or reviews, no part of this book may be reproduced in any manner without prior written permission from the publisher. Write: Permissions, Wipf and Stock Publishers, 199 W. 8th Ave., Suite 3, Eugene, OR 97401.

Pickwick Publications
An Imprint of Wipf and Stock Publishers
199 W. 8th Ave., Suite 3
Eugene, OR 97401

www.wipfandstock.com

PAPERBACK ISBN: 978-1-5326-4325-5
HARDCOVER ISBN: 978-1-5326-4326-2
EBOOK ISBN: 978-1-5326-4327-9

Cataloguing-in-Publication data:

Names: Thurmond-Malone, Myrna, author. | Yetunde, Pamela Ayo, foreword.

Title: Midwifing—a womanist approach to pastoral counseling : investigating the fractured self, slavery, violence, and the black woman / by Myrna Thurmond-Malone ; foreword by Pamela Ayo Yetunde.

Description: Eugene, OR: Pickwick Publications, 2019. | Includes bibliographical references.

Identifiers: ISBN 978-1-5326-4325-5 (paperback). | ISBN 978-1-5326-4326-2 (hardcover). | ISBN 978-1-5326-4327-9 (ebook).

Subjects: LCSH: Women--Pastoral counseling of. | Pastoral counseling. | Pastoral psychology. | Womanist theology.

Classification: BR563 T58 2019 (print). | BR563 (ebook).

Scripture quotations are taken from the New Revised Standard Version Bible, copyright © 1989 National Council of the Churches of Christ in the United States of America. Used by permission. All rights reserved worldwide.

Manufactured in the U.S.A.   06/13/19

In loving memory of my bradah, Al'Tericke Mitchell, whom I love with all my heart. He was my sunshine on raining days. I dedicate this book to him for keeping me smiling and laughing through the difficult moments of my life. Thank you for always having my back and loving me past my pain. He was the first good man in my life, the first man I trusted, and the first man I loved, and I will always cherish and honor his memory.

Contents

Foreword by Pamela Ayo Yetunde | ix
Preface | xiii
Acknowledgments | xvii

Introduction | 1
1. Historical Background | 9
2. Literature Review | 28
3. Theoretical and Theological Framework | 43
4. Research Methodology | 56
5. Research Findings | 62
6. Psychological, Sociocultural, and Theological Themes / Theological Reflection / Discussion of Discourse | 109
7. Conclusions | 126

Appendix A: IBR Protocol Proposal | 139
Appendix B: Prescreening Questions | 144
Appendix C: Consent Form | 145
Appendix D: Advertising Flyer | 149
Appendix E: Prescreening Interview Assessment Tool | 150
Appendix F: Prescreening Assessment Tool | 152
Glossary | 155
Bibliography | 159

Foreword

WE DO NOT EXIST without a birth, and we do not give birth without excruciating pain. Intense pain gets suppressed, lies dormant, becomes internalized, seeps sideways, or explodes in a surprising rush of rage *in order to be re-born again*. The cycles of our first birth and subsequent re-births, for African-American women in the context of the violent womb called the United States of America, is what Christian womanist pastoral psychotherapist Rev. Dr. Myrna Thurmond-Malone, wants her readers to understand—no matter how painful it is to arrive at that understanding. *Midwifing—A Womanist Approach to Pastoral Counseling: Investigating the Fractured Self, Slavery, Violence, and the Black Woman*, is a gentle, yet brutally honest guide into the lives of black women coming to grips with complex pain as well as new beginnings. Counselors interested in improving their counseling skills with African-American women might ask, "Is it necessary to bring all this pain?" Thurmond-Malone shows us the way to be with the intense pain that is unique to many African-American women's lived experiences.

Thurmond-Malone, having lived the life of the women in her study, knows the tendency Americans, including American pastoral psychotherapists, have to superficially skim the surfaces of American history when it comes to the centuries-long enslavement of Africans and their descendants. Thurmond-Malone challenges her readers, repeatedly, to face the facts of enslavement, including the repeated rapes, repeated pregnancies, selling off of children into slavery, genocide, turning darker-skinned and lighter-skinned African descended people against each other, and the desire to be white or pass for white, as ways America's peculiar institution of slavery has left its indelible cultural blot.

Through the intergenerational transmission of slave traumas in a society still largely bent on destroying black lives through imprisonment, policing, and citizen vigilantism, the peculiar institution of slavery still haunts African-descended women to this very day. It is as if Thurmond-Malone is saying that we must imagine, with all of our might, what it must have been like to be treated as a slave so that we counselors and psychotherapists can radically join our African-American women clients as midwives, creating a nurturing womb (the therapeutic space) within the violent womb (the US, the states, cities, towns, and households where we live), so that these women can be re-born into wholeness. Thurmond-Malone is asking us to examine our impulses to be skimmers of this sordid history rather than archeologists, non-stick Teflon rather than reflecting mirrors, innocent and distant bystanders rather than midwives, but it is easier to be a skimming Teflon bystander than it is to be an archeologist that mirrors and helps give birth. Thurmond-Malone is asking psychotherapists and counselors to dig deeper and deeper, empathize so intimately that we actually feel something, and with the care of a loving parent, prepare the therapeutic space for the gestation into wholeness. What is this midwifing method about?

Part of the midwifing method comes out of an African norm of interdependence. Midwifing for African-American women who have suffered racial and/or sexual trauma, is a group process, facilitated by an African-descended woman who refrains from judgment while inviting the unfolding of narratives kept hidden under the façade of the strong black woman myth. The therapeutic posture is one of radical hospitality, like the mother who says to her developing baby "My body is yours until you have your own." In other words, the womb she creates is for multiple re-births. How painful, yet how joyful! The facilitator needs to be very skilled in identifying projections, welcoming projections, receiving resentments, not taking insults personally, and facilitating so that everyone in the group participates in the re-births of themselves and each other. Midwifing is interdependent and communal—not your standard one-on-one model for achieving psychological wholeness, and the facilitating midwife has to have the capacity to give birth to a multitude while withstanding excruciating pain. Painful. Joyful.

Read *Midwifing* mindfully. Read *Midwifing* contemplatively. Imagine yourself as you are the women in this study and the Rev. Dr. Thurmond-Malone herself. Visualize what it is like to be ignored, violated, disrespected, isolated, and alienated while also being expected to care for others, especially the ones who oppress you, and you will get a sense of how the impact and expectations of slavery get played out in our lives today. *Midwifing* is a culturally-appropriate healing methodology to help recover the interdependence and communal aspects of African life that have been lost.

Pamela Ayo Yetunde, ThD
Assistant Professor, Pastoral Care and Counseling
Director, Interreligious Chaplaincy
United Theological Seminary of the Twin Cities

Preface

THE RESEARCH OUTLINED IN the following pages developed out of my passion for wellness, healing, and wholeness of black women. This topic is a direct result of my own journey to wellness, healing, and wholeness as a woman who experienced sexual, emotional, and physical abuse, as a clergyperson who has experienced racism and sexism, and as a career professional and student who experienced institutional and societal racism, sexism, and classism in Western society.

Throughout my faith journey, God, music, creativity, education, family, and sisterhood have allowed me to cope with my experiences. During my seminary education I learned that I had not dealt with the experience of sexual violence and oppression, but in fact had suppressed them in order to function in society. I experienced what educator, pastoral theologian, and counselor Archie Smith Jr. terms "bleed through."[1] Smith asserts that "pentimento" occurs when the past is not dealt with but forgotten or covered over.[2] Smith's framework and use of the term provided an awareness that led me to seek help and uncover the parts of my experience that I was covering over in order to function in society. In addition, the work of Dr. Joy DeGruy, in her book *Post Traumatic Slave Syndrome: America's Legacy of Enduring Injury and Healing*, deals with the embodiment of intergenerational trauma. The traumatic experiences that enslaved Africans and African Americans experienced pre and post slavery. DeGruy writes, "Trauma is an injury caused by an outside, usually violent force, event or experienced . . . it can distort our attitudes and beliefs . . . [which] can result in dysfunctional behaviors . . . [and] impact

---

1. Smith, *Relational Self*, x.

2. Pentimento is the technique of removing the top layer of paint to reveal a painting underneath. Smith uses the term as a means of "covering up a canvas previously painted," causing the experiences of their life to "bleed through."

an individual's DNA, and the manifestation of the traumas . . . can be passed along genetically to future offspring.[3]

During my research I discovered there were not enough adequate spaces for Black women to lament, uncover, and deal with their past. Moreover, during my own personal journey I uncovered how my past was bleeding into my present and my embodiment of trauma was not just what I personally experienced, but my maternal ancestors. My journey of healing and wholeness occurred when I learned of womanist theology and pastoral care. This was the gateway for me to explore identity and wholeness and its impact of personhood. Furthermore, I was introduced to a wonderful womanist pastoral counselor who created a safe space for me to cry out and acknowledge my experiences and re-author my story. Thus, I was guided to discover my voice and subsequent identity and healing as a victim survivor, leading me today, to research why black women suffer and how they use their faith and relationship with God to cope and ponder other ways of coping, thereby moving them from surviving to thriving. Lastly, to reclaim my past and move toward my future, this concept is known as Sankofa.[4]

I began this exploration with the enslaved ancestors of our past and black women of today, exploring stereotypes and overall wellness of black women. This, in turn, led me to investigate the impact of black women's experiences of violence and oppression on their identity. It was my personal journey that led me here, but it was the voices of other black women that created an interest to further investigate how the experiences of black women are unique and how they need safe and sacred spaces to lament, deconstruct negative images, and re-author their narratives.

I witnessed black women tell their stories of violence and oppression for the first time. I listened as they lamented to one another and witnessed as they provided safety for each other in the telling of their stories. I later learned that it was my presence, response, commitment, and interest in their stories that created safety and an opportunity for them to hear their stories, even if for the first time. The subsequent sessions demonstrated the power of support—thus, leading me to explore further my notion of midwifery and how it created a sense of safety for enslaved women as they birthed their children in the midst of violence and oppression. Using midwifery as a metaphor, I, therefore, began the investigation into the

---

3. DeGruy, *Post Traumatic Slave*, 14.
4. DeGruy, *Post Traumatic Slave*, 7.

lived reality of African American women and my therapeutic model that I call midwifing.

The introduction will invite readers to learn of the unique experiences of black women, following with a historical lens of slavery, thus leading to my midwifing approach as a means of creating a safe space for healing.

Acknowledgements

I WOULD LIKE TO thank those who provided me with unconditional love, support, encouragement, and guidance throughout each phase of my journey. The prayers, words of wisdom, and mentorship allowed me the opportunity to stretch myself and explore the deeper parts of myself throughout each chapter in my life that has shaped me into the woman I have become.

A special thank you to my midwives, my mother Mary, sister Myriam, aunt Shirley, aunt Marie, aunt Bop, aunt Rose, sister friends Jackie, Alisha, Ayo, Brandy, Quanika, Carolyn, and my Womanist community. Thank you for creating safe and sacred holding spaces for me to lament. Your guidance, support, affirmation, and nurturing helped me to become liberated and empowered to claim my voice and walk into my destiny with boldness.

Thank you to Drs. Pamela Cooper-White, Emanuel Lartey, Carolyn McCrary, and Edward Wimberly for your guidance, wisdom, and encouragement.

Finally, to my husband Darcy, daughters Fontashia and Jacqueline, and my son Asante, I'm grateful for your love, support, and understanding during this process. To the African-American women clinical research group participants who experienced forms of racism, sexism, and classism. Thank you for the courage and strength that allowed you to push past the oppression and tell your story. Your voice will offer hope to others who are silenced. I pray that you continue to tell your story, embrace your identity, and walk into your destiny.

Introduction

I was bused to a White school and was the first Black person to segregate the school.... I remember them lined up so I couldn't enter and was hit with rocks.... It was so bad my parents took me out of the school.

—Karen

Violence represents an infringement on human rights and the rights of creation. This dehumanizing experience is intrusive, destroys creativity and one's inner essence, is rife with abuse and prohibits one's freedom.

—Cheryl Kirk-Duggan, *Misbegotten Anguish*

To defile [Black women] is to treat [them] which is sacred as if [they] were base, to deem [them] as less than [creating an identity of worthlessness].... [The] sin of American patriarchy ... [was and is] the defilement of Black women's bodies and the resulting attack upon their spirits and self-esteem constitutes the gravest kind of social sin.

—Phyllis Isabella Sheppard, *Self, Culture, and Others*

The violence perpetrated against black women is unique. It needs to be explored separately from violence experienced by white women. This in no way diminishes the experience of violence toward white women. However, I am attempting to lift up the experiences of black women and highlight what I have termed their "multiple-reality experience." I define this as the injurious experience of slavery, domestication, dehumanization, racism, classism, and sexism against their mental, emotional, and physical health. This anguish was perpetrated on black women by white men, white women, and black men, and created a unique suffering experience. Examples of harmful experiences related to the multiple-reality experiences of black women can be seen through stories of the group participants portrayed in the book. There are Abbie and Tanya, who shared the pain and hurt from being called ugly, monkey, blackie, big nose, big lips, and nappy headed, Olivia, who shared her continued struggle with being black—"I just want to be identified as Christian"—and Dianne, who states, "I don't know who I am," as she struggled with her experience of sexual abuse by her brother. An examination of their overall narratives created a presumption that there was a deeper implication and raised questions regarding the connection of African descendant person's experiences of slavery and how that impacted and shaped their identity as black women. As each group participant shared variables of their narrative, the remnants and consequences of slavery could readily be identified, and it could be seen how they may have played a role in their anguish and created a fracturing within their mental and emotional state and the embodiment of trauma passed down from one generation to the next.

Within the outline of the book you will be able to examine slavery and the violence that black female slaves suffered from their white masters. Also how black male slaves were forced to participate in acts of rape, creating an abusive internal structure as black male slaves participated in the violence against slave women. The study also looks at the witness of other forms of forceful and aggressive behavior toward African female slaves within the slave community.

Within my writing, I refer to slavery in the United States as a system of more than ownership. American slavery was an organized system that created economic wealth and privilege for whites through the selling of a commodity (Africans) and the creating of a product (children—Black, mixed, and slave children). American slavery stole the humanity of Africans and their descendants, and instilled within their psyches a loss of freedom, humanity, and identity. Enslaved Africans were brainwashed and indoctrinated to see themselves as their captors identified them—a non-human product without freedom or spirit. Moreover, this loss of freedom and humanity meant the denial of culture, heritage, language, and identity. In other words, American slavery was a form of religion and methodology with the goal of dehumanizing and controlling the minds, bodies, and spirits of the enslaved.

INTRODUCTION

Slavery can be understood as a religion and methodology as it developed a set of particular beliefs and practices that (1) instilled in the enslaved and the enslaver that those who were enslaved were not human, (2) designed rituals such as hanging, whipping, mutilation, rape, and other inhumane acts of violence that were designed to keep those enslaved under the submission and obedience of their masters as if the master was their god, and (3) deliberately sought to strip the enslaved of their identity, culture, language, family, and heritage in order that the enslaver might reign as superior and maintain those enslaved to be without humanity.

A study of the structure of slavery makes space to explore the understanding of selves who were forced to relate to other human beings who enslaved, raped and dehumanized other persons supported by religion. However, I do not intend to focus on the mind of the enslaver. Rather, I focus on how these minds and persons created an understanding and view of African and African American women. Additionally, I will explore how the structured system of oppression, including racism, sexism, and classism, was solidified throughout slavery and created remnants that resulted in the creation of black women's identity today by self, community, and society as a whole. Which can be considered as a disruption of their narrative explored in "Trauma and the Historical Turn in Black Literary Discourse" by Aida Levy-Hussen.[1]

This examination on the impact of violence against black women who have to deal with the internalization of patriarchy (sexism) and racism is useful to black women who have experienced violence. Additionally, it addresses class issues due to the disproportionate number of African American women who are poor, compared with the general population, and their resulting inability to access care. Although men are not a part of the research population, there are indirect implications as well for black men who have perpetrated violence against black women. Finally, the writer seeks to speak to women's use of spirituality, not traditional modes of therapy, to deal with their pain.

This analysis into the history of slavery and its legacy of violence attempts to explain why African American women would need a therapist who is sensitive to their multiple-reality experience, and how a therapist's awareness of this experience could provide a safe space within the therapeutic encounter to allow women to disarm and lament. It also highlights the importance of qualified, culturally competent therapists who understand

---

1. Levy-Hussen, "Trauma and the Historical Turn," 196.

the multiple-reality experience and can access the internalized shame that some African American women may carry regarding their selves, which may contribute to the development of a fractured self and makes space to examine and recognize the embodiment of intergenerational trauma.

A cultural awareness is important due to cultural countertransference which is made up of deeply held, unconsciously motivated learnings about race, sexuality, class, ethnicity, gender, and various other physical markers of social location that often stereotype black women. My usage of the term intends to suggest that the cultural countertransference that emerges in response to black female bodies, sexualities, and identity is dynamic.[2] To gain insight into the fullness of the development and understanding of self, there must be an awareness and understanding of the legacy of slavery.

Finally, therapists also need to understand the role of spirituality within the lives of African American women and how they have coped with violence (racism, sexism, and classism). The importance of understanding the unique experience of black women has been noted by womanist scholars such as Carol Watkins Ali who states:

> The womanist tradition . . . seeks to eradicate paternalism, racism, sexism, classism, or any kind of oppression. . . . [We speak and identify] God as a divine co-sufferer . . . [therefore pastoral psychology] needs to understand the psychological implications of being African and American . . . [and] find ways to equip and empower African Americans psychologically to resist and cope.[3]

The idea of womanist was derived from womanism, which was coined in 1982 by African American author and activist Alice Walker in her book, *In Search of Our Mothers' Gardens*.[4]

There are several therapeutic goals when counseling African American women. First, they need to deconstruct the inner shame they may carry as a result of racism, sexism, and classism. Second, the counselee must re-define what it means to be a strong black woman by exploring the question: Do strong black women just accept violence and men's abuse of power because it is just so, or do strong black women allow themselves to feel and lament hurt and pain? A third therapeutic goal is to identify ways of coping with life other than spirituality. Spirituality is a significant way of coping, but not the only way. Can a strong black woman possess

2. Crumpton, *Crafting*, 128.
3. Watkins Ali, *Survival Liberation*, 7.
4. Walker, *Search Mothers Gardens*.

diverse healthy ways to cope and still be spiritual? Finally, therapy needs to provide an awareness that can help African American women move from a fractured self—the breaking of one's mental, emotional, and spiritual self as a result of inhumane treatment, dehumanization, oppression, objectification (sexual and non-sexual), and domestication that has cost women their freedom of voice, freedom of interpretation, freedom to choose, freedom of personhood, and freedom—to develop and become a true self so that they can re-integrate and deconstruct their multiple-reality experience. These goals can, in turn, empower women to speak their truth and become whole in mind, body, and soul. I believe this will allow them to explore their lived reality and life experiences that were formed out of oppression and move them to a place of self-acceptance that values their identity and humanity as black women.

Thus, my work focuses on how healing and wholeness can occur as black women receive adequate care through a culturally empathic therapeutic encounter with a pastoral counselor willing to hear women's stories through their own lenses, to affirm their narratives, and to facilitate the deconstruction of negative stereotypes. In so doing, the therapist creates a safe and sacred space for women to become unarmored and lament—moving from a fractured self to a whole self that embraces their humanity.

The sanctioning of violence toward some African American women has had an impact on their identity, fostering negative identifications of black women and creating brokenness. This negative history has impacted how some black women's view of themselves and how society and others view and treat them. Although the impact of violence resulting from racism, sexism, and classism affects black women differently, research on the subject points to a commonality of the harmful effects on the psyche and development of some black women, which recently research illustrates the intergenerational trauma that can be embodied from one generation to the next. And it has created a generational misconception of the identity, value, and worth of black women.

This generational misconception became a concern for this author through the hearing of black women's stories infused with low self-esteem, hopelessness, lack of identity, stereotypes, and shame, and their struggle to release and lament their suffering and pain. In addition, many black women have suffered negative counseling experiences that merely compound their pain. Past therapists' lack of understanding and the women's subsequent feelings of judgment have caused them to arm themselves, rather than to be transparent and feel safe in their need for receiving care and expressing lament.

In Charisse Jones's and Kumea Shorter-Gooden's *Shifting: The Double Lives of Black Women in America*, the authors explore the complex reality of black women in the United States—what they explore as the shifting, ever changing positioning and reality of black women as they maneuver through their experiences of oppression and violence and the impact it has on their psyche. Jones and Shorter-Gooden describe how many black women break down emotionally or physically under the pressure, their lives stripped of joy and unable to withstand the onslaught of negative messages. They become susceptible to an array of psychological problems. For example, in a National Center for Health Statistics study of more than 43,000 adults in the United States, black women were three times as likely as white men and twice as likely as white women to have experienced distressing feelings. In the study they lamented how hard it is for them to express and accept their own disappointments and vulnerabilities.

The pressure to maintain the image of the strong black woman creates a tremendous facade.[5] The multiple-reality experience of black women impacts their wellness and identity. I believe that black women desire to take off the facade and reframe the image of the strong black women. However, safe and sacred spaces where they are able to lament and express their concerns, pain, vulnerabilities, and everyday life stressors are limited. And while the discussion of the plight of the black woman has been explored in the past, I aim not to focus on the resiliency of black women, but on the need for conducive spaces and approaches to create safe and healing places for their voices and mirroring different ways to identify as "strong black woman" that positions them to forego the outward image and focus on their internal identity.

> It's time to stop bleeding.... The past bleeds through after it has been forgotten, willfully suppressed, or covered over by the present.... When the past is forgotten and covered over by newer interpretations of the self and ... working society, then unresolved and past traumatic experiences begin to bleed through [and healing doesn't occur].
>
> —Archie Smith Jr. and Ursula Riedel-Pfaefflin,
> *Siblings by Choice*

---

5. Jones et al., *Shifting*, 8–11.

INTRODUCTION

In creating safe and sacred spaces for black women to stop bleeding and explore what has been internalized and covered up, I will explore this question: How can black women heal from injurious and harmful values based in slavery (dehumanization, domestication, racism /white supremacy, classism, and sexism) that have been internalized by African American women and have fostered the creation of a fractured self? Sub-questions that are also essential to this study are

1. How do some black women become fragmented?
2. How does this fragmentation hinder them in the world and impact their ability to build healthy relationships and a healthy self-identity?
3. What external factors in their lived reality foster this fragmented identification of self?

The term "multiple reality" will refer to the diverse experiences of racism, sexism, and classism as forms of violence experienced by black women that may lead to the subsequent fragmentation. That fragmentation will be explored throughout this research project. Fragmentation, for this author, is the emotional and spiritual internal breaking of the black woman that occurs when she is constantly silenced, dismissed, negated, violated, devalued, and defined as worthless through the lenses of those who perpetrate violence against her humanity.

In chapter one, I argue that slavery established consequences of dehumanization, domestication, objectification, racism, sexism, and classism. These birthed an epidemic of violence that constructed a negative framework in the black women's identity. Further, I examine the same construct, drawing on ethnography as a qualitative research method, utilizing womanist, Kohutian, and African-centered psychological theories to bring understanding and to articulate the multidimensional reality of black women's experience in the United States.

Violence has been a part of black women's experience in America for many generations on multiple levels, beginning with malicious acts of violence in slavery. The multigenerational experience of black women who experienced and continue to experience violence shapes their perception of self, prior to and/or after the act(s) of violence. Moreover, the legacy of slavery remains for black women through their experiences of dehumanization, domestication, objectification, racism, sexism, and classism. These factors shape the way they view and identify themselves. Therefore, I attempt to explore the normality of black women's experiences interwoven with racism, sexism, and classism and how these experiences have shaped the fractured self of the black woman's identity. Throughout this book I use "black" and "African American" interchangeably.

1

Historical Background

Emancipation did little to protect black women from sexual victimization. No longer the property of a particular white slaveholder, freed black women were vulnerable to sexual assault by any white man.

—Bernadette J. Brooten and Jacqueline L. Hazelton,
Beyond Slavery

Slavery was just moments away . . . women . . . survived the auction block, involuntary separation from their families, and . . . being raped by white men. Mrs. Smith [a midwife after the emancipation recalls her experiences in Greene County, one of Alabama's known lands of slavery], too, experienced deep suffering and discontent.

—Margaret Charles Smith and Linda Janet Holmes,
Listen to Me Good

THE EXPERIENCES OF BLACK women are unique and need to be lifted up in order to highlight and acknowledge their experience. Black women have been forcefully removed from their homeland and enslaved. They have been dehumanized and domesticated. They have experienced racism, sexism, and classism. In addition to all of this, they have suffered mental, emotional, and physical violence and abuse perpetrated against minds, bodies, and souls by white men, white women, and black men. To gain insight into black women's normality and psychological development, I begin by providing descriptions of the effects of slavery, dehumanization, domestication, racism, sexism, and classism, utilizing several voices of men and women who have also studied the experience of black women.

The remnants (legacy) of slavery can be seen in the negative identification of black women for whom I have provided counseling, care, and mentorship. Their fracturing appears to be fused with a lack of identity and/or the embracing of the identity placed on them by others. The self-hatred that emerges through the narratives of many black women points to the legacy and history of violence. A concept that voices this experience is *maafa*. *Maafa* is the genocide of Africans and their descendants during and after slavery. To provide greater insight into *maafa*, I will highlight scholars and pastoral theologians' voices to lift up how it has impacted the identity of black women (although men were also affected). Scholar Makungu M. Akinyela, who explores the consequences of slavery and its influence on black women's normality, writes:

> The *maafa* concept explains the condition of disorganization, disunity, self-hatred, and alienation affecting African people. . . . *Maafa*, or great destruction, is a Ki-Swahili word that is culturally distinct, self-determined naming of the genocide experienced by Africans under Western colonialism and slavery. . . . *Maafa* is an apt description of African enslavement and the after effects of Jim Crow, white supremacy, and racism as a source of much of the emotional stress that affects black people.[1]

Pastoral theologian Lee Butler describes *maafa* as "ranging from maiming to murder . . . those degrading and dehumanizing experiences have caused us [African Americans] to feel isolation, despair and rage."[2] Continuing from that perspective, womanist pastoral theologian Carol Watkins Ali writes, "In light of the dehumanizing treatment of blacks physically and psychologically during slavery . . . its aim was to brainwash the slave, destroy the mind, and replace it with the mind of the master. . . . A slave would have no sense of himself/herself that was separate from the self the master wanted him/her to have."[3]

A critical construct of *maafa* for this researcher is its aim to dehumanize African Americans. This paper also endeavors to examine how the denial of *maafa*'s aim continues today and remains a means of oppression and violence against the minds, bodies, and souls of African American women (and men), impacting the psychological development and identification of self. Lastly, in "Lifting the Veil: The Shoah and the Maafa in Conversation,"

---

1. Akinyela, "Wake Destruction."
2. Butler, *Liberating Our Dignity*, 209.
3. Watkins Ali, *Survival Liberation*, 71.

HISTORICAL BACKGROUND

Brad Braxton explains that the violence experienced by the descendants of those enslaved from West Africa was so great, a term was created to speak to their experience, highlighting the destructiveness and impact of chattel slavery. Braxton writes:

> During the two and a half centuries of chattel slavery, millions of Africans were physically mutilated, sexually violated, and ultimately murdered by a multi-national political and economic system with a voracious appetite for the sugar and cotton produced in those 'concentration camps' called plantations. The physical and psychic rupture of slavery upon the global community was, and is, so dramatic that a special term had to be created, "The Great Disaster."[4]

In slavery, black women were used as objects by white women, to be their domestic servants (wet nurse, cook, and mammy to the white children), and as sexual objects by their husbands, other white men, and black slave men. Micki McElya, author of *Clinging to Mammy: The Faithful Slave in Twentieth-Century America*, writes, "The institution of slavery was wracked with sexual depravity and the rape and concubinage of black women by white men."[5] McElya describes how black slave women's physical attributes were seen as opposites of the desirable, white femininity. This image, created in the minds of white captors, allowed them to violently sexualize black women slaves, father black women's children, and continue the cycle of domestication of their mixed and/or mulatto children. Moreover, white women's use of the term "mammy," even after the end of American slavery, allowed them to continue in the fantasy that black women were still their slaves. David P. Geggus, author of *Slave and Free Colored Women in St. Dominique*, describes the horrible acts of violence toward female slaves at the hands of their white captors as "vicious sadism."[6]

In *Wounds of the Spirit: Black Women, Violence and Resistance Ethics*, Traci West examines the exploitation of black women in America. Beginning with the dehumanizing brutality of chattel slavery within the United States, West lifts up slave and contemporary narratives to give an account of a long history of injury imposed on the minds, bodies and souls of African American women:

---

4. Braxton, "Lifting Veil," 286.
5. McElya, *Clinging to Mammy*, 8.
6. Geggus, "Slave," 265.

> Slave women lived with the threat of sexual violence whether they worked in the master's house or in the fields. White masters, white overseers, and black drivers raped slave women. They also faced forms of sexual violence that were the peculiar inventions of the slave system ... as 'forced breeders' were made to submit to sexual relations with black slave men ... [additionally] sexualized torture for slaves was the practice of whipping pregnant women and beating nursing mothers ... [so] severely that blood and milk flowed simultaneously from their breast.[7]

Another remnant of slavery injurious to black women resulting from sexual exploitation is described by psychologist Nancy Boyd-Franklin, who writes:

> Sexual exploitation on the part of the white slave master resulted in many 'mulatto' or light skinned children. ... One of the consequences of the system of slavery. ... Black families have identified with the dominant society and incorporated some of the prejudices of the majority white culture. All African Americans, irrespective of their color, shade, darkness or lightness are aware from a very early age that their blackness makes them different.[8]

Today, black women continue to deal with the questions "What is beauty?" "Am I beautiful?" Pulitzer Prize–winning author Toni Morrison, in *The Bluest Eye*, explores those questions. Pecola Breedlove, a darkskinned character who deemed herself ugly because of her skin was also deemed ugly in her home, school, and community. One day she fell victim to teasing by black boys who judged her because of the color of her skin. Morrison writes, "A group of boys was circling and holding at bay a victim, Pecola Breedlove ... thrilled by the easy power of a majority, they gaily harassed her. Black e mo, black e mo ... their exquisitely learned self-hatred ... for their own sake, they were prepared to sacrifice [her] to the flaming pit."[9] Morrison portrays young black boys who identified with the dominant society, internalized self-hatred, and, in turn, tormented Pecola through their own racist acts of violence.

Merril Smith, in the *Encyclopedia of Rape*, investigates the dual contradictory system that was established by slavery for black women.

She writes:

7. West, *Wounds Spirit*, 14–15.
8. Boyd-Franklin, *Black Families*, 7.
9. Morrison, *Bluest Eye*, 55.

> Slavery created a dual and contradictory system.... Southern law reinforced the protection of white women as property, while justifying the sexual exploitation of black women. White slaveholders held absolute power over their slave population and could rape their slaves at will without fear of punishment. The systematic sexual exploitation of black female slaves and their mulatto offspring reveals a society weighed down by public and private violence. Rape laws did not apply or protect black slaves [and after slavery] from the abuses of their masters. Instead, these women shouldered the double burden of their gender and race.[10]

The violence that plagued the bodies and minds of enslaved black women would be considered a crime against humanity—but black women were not seen as human. They were, instead, understood to be and treated as property, and as a product that reproduces. Black enslaved females had no power over their stories, bodies, children or selves. Instead, the black female slave was supposed to take and accept whatever the white master, white woman, and black man imposed on her. The white master imposed his God, language, culture, and sexual objectification, while the white mistress imposed upon her the role of domestic servant. The dominant society imposed its idea of "beauty" and "lady." Black women throughout history have been treated and portrayed as less than ladies, and many black men continue this legacy by reinforcing the negative effects of slavery through physical, emotional, and spiritual abuse and oppressive violence toward black women.

The injustice and continued violence that have been inflicted upon black women as white men raped black women with impunity can be seen within the lives of black women today and their continued struggle to gain power and freedom over their own bodies and identity.[11] Furthermore, images projected on black women (Jezebel, matriarch) and the use of the mammy construct served to whitewash the violence and sexual exploitation that was done to the bodies and minds of black women.

Womanist pastoral theologian Phillis Sheppard describes the black woman's body as her text. She argues that one must gain understanding of the construct of the black female body as a historical text.[12] Similarly, professor of law and sociology Dorothy Roberts asserts, "One of the most horrific aspects of slavery's ownership of black bodies was enslaved women's experience of sexual exploitation by white men.... Slavery put black women's body on

---

10. Smith, *Encyclopedia*, 235.
11. Mabunda, *Contemporary*, 264.
12. Sheppard, *Self, Culture*, 151.

display . . . [and] sexual exploitation of enslaved women generated a degrading iconography of black female sexuality designed to legitimate White men's immorality."[13] Likewise, black men who raped black girls during slavery were excused because no law recognized unwanted sex between male and female slaves as rape (George v. State of Mississippi, 1895). Roberts states, "When a slave named George was charged with having sex with a child under the age of ten, a Mississippi court dismissed the indictment on the grounds that 'the crime of rape does not exist in this State between African slaves. . . . [Furthermore,] laws regulating sex among whites [were not] relevant to slaves [and] left it to be regulated by their owners.'"[14]

Darnell Moore looks at how black bodies speak, emote, and remember as he examines the black body as a map or "walking text."[15] Moreover, he sheds light on how, from this perspective, healing is slow due to traumatic experiences of trauma on the black body. Robert Allen, author of *Black Awakening*, spoke these words during a speech on domestic violence, "It is a tragedy that some of us have internalized the violence of their racist/sexist society and brought it into our communities and homes. . . . But this can never justify transforming hurt into rage and violence against Black women's bodies and spirits."[16] Ultimately, slavery aided in the lasting foundation of the contemporary notion regarding black women's bodies and sexuality; and the sexual gratification of white and black men continues to plague black women even at the cost of their own mental and emotional health.[17] Thus, one can see how the black woman's body is her historical text, and from a womanist view it raises the question, "What does her body have to teach and inform us about the significance and uniqueness of her story"?

Today, black women continue to be objectified and exploited long after legalized slavery has ended. They continue to be degraded and treated as objects for the sexual gratification of men. Stereotypical images of "Jezebel," an oversexed black woman, can be heard and seen in music, television, movies, and other media. Patricia Hill Collins exploration of white superiority and comparison of the use of stereotypes to dehumanize and sexualize black women and their bodies gives light to Jezebel, mammy, and other derogatory stereotypes that have been used to identify black

13. Roberts, "Paradox Silence," 43–44.
14. Roberts, "Paradox Silence," 44.
15. Moore, "Theorizing Black Body," 175–88.
16. Carillo et al., 111.
17. Roberts, "Paradox Silence," 43.

women.[18] Black women often are presented as promiscuous, immoral, sluttish, lustful, evil, welfare queens, hoochie, freaks, bitches, castrating, and hoodrats—to name just a few derogatory images. Besides being degraded in media and other entertainment, they are also stigmatized within their community and society. And these stereotypes discourage black women from reporting violence against their bodies today.

Research, such as that recorded by Roxanne Donovan, has shown that black girls and women in high school and college who have experienced so-called date rape are less likely to report the incident, because they often do not view it as rape. Instead, they believe they were responsible and/or caused the exploitation and violence against their bodies.[19] Additionally, black women receive less empathy and support as a result of these negative stereotypes and their shapely bodies.[20] Black women are subjugated by stereotypes that make them more likely to experience violence, and plagued by a system that frequently re-victimizes them when they seek help.[21] This assertion, illustrated by Donovan in her article entitled, "To Blame or Not to Blame: Influences of Target Race and Observer Sex On Rape Blame Attribution," has been voiced in therapy sessions and mentoring sessions with young and seasoned black women with whom I have had the pleasure of working, as they shared their experiences of intimate violence (i.e., sexual violation, rape, molestation, and sexual and physical assault by white and black men). The repeated themes of their silence echo as if their voice and pain do not matter: "But who is going to believe me?"; "I'm just a black woman." And there is the resounding reiteration of "I just have to deal with it, what doesn't break me makes me stronger." Throughout my work in church ministry and pastoral counseling, those words have resonated in my ear.

Beth Richie explores the correlation between racism, sexism, classism, and black women's experiences of violence and re-victimization. In *Arrested Justice: Black Women, Violence and America's Prison Nation*, Richie asserts:

> The impact of stereotypes, stigma, and marginalized identities extends far beyond the realm of creating emotional and social circumstances for black women that leaves them vulnerable to male violence . . . [and] contemporary media images contribute to the emotional manipulation of black women. One need only look at

---

18. Collins, *Black Sexual Politics*, 28.
19. Donovan, "To Blame," 723.
20. Donovan, "To Blame," 723.
21. Donovan, "To Blame," 723

the portrayal of black women in cultural venues like music videos, movies, and novels. The primary culprit is surely the mainstream entertainment industry controlled by capitalist markets that are by and large owned by white men.[22]

Moreover, Richie points to effects of violence in low income black communities, including a distrust of systems. This and other perspectives illustrate the long history of sexual exploitation and violence on the bodies, minds, and souls of black women, as well as racial stereotypes that silence their voices and further fragment the self. Lastly, an example of the stereotype of black women as sexual objects can be interpreted through the actions of police officer Daniel Ken Holtzclaw who raped, stalked, and sexually assaulted seven African American women while on duty—another example of injustice through the misuse of power.

When the history of violence towards black women is explored it provides insight into the damaging and continuous impact of oppressive violence experienced by black women, and allows therapists to explore the multigenerational transmission process that may be applicable to clients' experience of violence. Psychiatrist and early family systems thinker Murray Bowen writes that the multigenerational transmission process means that those who emerge with lower levels [of differentiation (i.e., Bowen's primary measure for maturity)] have been exposed to more than an average number of life's misfortunes and those who emerge with higher levels of differentiation have had more of life's good fortunes. The fortunes and misfortunes are defined by the family emotional process rather than by the usual advantages as defined by society.[23]

Similarly, Rabbi Edwin Friedman, another family systems thinker, describes multigenerational transmission as "the presence of the past in the present moment. . . . A continuous natural process, with each generation pressing up against the next so that the past and present almost become a false dichotomy."[24] The perspectives of Bowen and Friedman provide an opportunity for further research to explore these experiences and acts of violence, and their impact, on the fractured self of the black woman's identity, which I will examine throughout the book.

Author, activist, and scholar Charlotte Pierce-Baker explores the stories of black women and young girls who have been raped and remained silent

---

22. Richie, *Arrested Justice*, 46.
23. Nyengele, *African Women's Theology*, 133.
24. Nyengele, *African Women's Theology*, 133.

about their experiences. Her book, *Surviving the Silence: Black Women's Stories of Rape*, is based on interviews in which she invited women to reflect on their experience and silence, as well as feeling that they were not free to speak against sexual exploitation of their own bodies. Experiences of violence perpetrated against the minds, bodies, and souls of black women can contribute to brokenness. Womanist pastoral theologian Carolyn McCrary describes black women's internalization of violence and suffering as brokenness. This brokenness, she says, has established unhealthy attitudes that impact the personhood of African American women. In "The Wholeness of Women," McCrary writes, "the intent is to explore the meaning of wholeness of women given life under oppressive structures also that oppressive values lead to unhealthy attitudes which impact generations and understanding of self."[25] McCrary notes that oppressive systems that support racism and sexism, and foster systemic oppression, result in unhealthy attitudes within self. Moreover, systemic oppression internalized by African and African American women creates an inward feeling of weakness. But McCrary argues that this weakness can be deconstructed when said systems are rejected. Casting down unhealthy attitudes stimulated and formed by violence (racism and sexism) allows black women to develop healthy attitudes about the self, to restore the self, and build healthier relationships.

McCrary provides a womanist framework to view, understand, and respond to violence against African and African American women by white men, white women, and black men. She seeks to move toward wholeness by acknowledging the pain of violence and developing a holistic, communal perspective. She postulates that to reach the goal of helping women recapture a state of inner wholeness, women must claim a healthy understanding of themselves.[26]

McCrary writes:

> Internalization ensure(s) that violence against women is continual; there is no opportunity to affirm the self as worthy and healthy. So, women in a desperate struggle to 'have peace' or to 'make peace' in 'bad' (anxiety producing) external relationships often suffer an internal, basically unconscious, raging war; their inner wholeness becomes a casualty to unjust and too often ill-intentioned demands on their personhood. Such fracturing is the

---

25. McCrary, "Wholeness," 260–61.
26. McCrary, "Wholeness," 276, 293.

damage done to women by the unjust and violent systems of racism and sexism.[27]

Deconstructing their negative identification of self-resulting from systems of violence will aide in their healing, and provide the opportunity for them to become whole. Examining their experiences can help black women to end the violence that continues to plague them long after both the end of slavery, and more than thirty years after the implementation of formal programs to address violence against women, such as the National Coalition Against Domestic Violence, the Institute on Domestic Violence in the African American Community, and the Battered Women's Justice Project, to name a few.

Violence

In this section I outline some of the factors impinging upon the wholeness of black women, including violence, sexism, racism, and classism. In this book I will explore violence from a Fanonian perspective as described and defined in Frantz Fanon's *The Wretched of the Earth*, and as used by Hussein Abdilahi Bulhan in *The Psychology of Oppression*. Fanon's lived experience allowed him to critique narrow interpretations of violence and lift up ways in which violence harmed the whole being of a person and society as a whole. His scrutiny builds a multidimensional approach to understanding and interpreting violence, whether intentional or non-intentional, by looking at violence as personal, institutional, and structural, and by considering the role of the colonizer and effects on the colonized. Bulhan explores the multiple-reality of violence according to Fanon's perspective, as well how persons of color and those who are non-white have internalized violence. Bulhan illustrates how each type of violence has oppression and inhumanity at its core.

He writes:

> Violence is any relation, process, or condition by which an individual or group violates the physical, social, and/or psychological integrity of another person or group. First violence is not simply an isolated physical act or a discrete random event. It is relation, process, and condition undermining, exploiting, and curtailing the well-being of the victim. Second, these violations are not simply moral or ethical, but also physical, social, and/or psychological. They involve demonstrable assault or injury of and damage to

27. McCrary, "Wholeness," 276.

the victim. Third, violence in any of the three domains—physical, social or psychological—has significant repercussions in the other two domains. Fourth, violence occurs not only between individuals, but also between groups and societies. Fifth, intention is less critical than consequence in most forms of violence. Any relation, process, or condition imposed by someone that injures the health and wellbeing of others is by definition violent.[28]

Exploring violence in this framework provides an opportunity to speak to the multiple-reality of experiences of black women. Furthermore, Bulhan describes how oppressive violence was exemplified in the master-slave relationship. He writes, "Slavery in fact reeked with violence in its crudest forms. A society founded on the exploitation of slaves was the crudest form of structural violence. The use of white militia to search out runaway black slaves exemplifies undisguised institutional violence. The omnipresent whip not only symbolized authority, but also ritualized interpersonal violence."[29] Bulhan also describes white men's historical freedom to rape black women. He illustrates a resulting intrapersonal violence by describing how Africans flung themselves into the Atlantic Ocean and committed suicide on plantations to escape their white captors. Bulhan sheds light on violence toward African Americans, but further exploration is needed to gain insight into the depth of oppressive violence that black women, in particular, have encountered personally, institutionally, and structurally. Although Bulhan discusses internalized violence resulting from oppressive violence outside one's personhood, he has not offered a more in-depth look at the internalized legacies of slavery, dehumanization, domestication, racism, sexism, and classism, as violence and how these have shaped the fractured selves of black women.

The violence experienced by enslaved women ranged from emotional to physical and sexual. The physical and emotional violence was experienced in the raping, lynching, and killing of other slaves. The use of public humiliation was seen in beatings, hangings, chains, mutilation, starvation, and imprisonment to name a few forms of violence black women experienced during and after slavery.[30]

The coercive sexual violence against black women during slavery was inevitable. The violence of rape and sexual depravity was encountered by

---

28. Bulhan, *Psychology Oppression*, 135.
29. Bulhan, *Psychology Oppression*, 156.
30. Healey, *Race, Ethnicity, Gender*, 111–12.

young and old Africans and African descendants during and after slavery. An example of this violence can be learned in the story of Celia who was purchased in 1850 at age fourteen by a Missouri farmer named Robert Newson. Celia was raped repeatedly by Mr. Newson for five years and bore his children. Her voice and humanity were stripped from her until one day Celia fought back and killed Mr. Newson. For his crime against her she received no justice and for her years of repeated rape she was sentenced by a Missouri court in 1855 to death by hanging.[31]

Violence towards black women was a sign of normality in white culture during and after slavery. Their cries went unheard and their tears unseen. Slavery in the US was much more than a source of economic wealth. It was an influential and forceful system of violence perpetrated against the minds, bodies, and souls of black women (and men). Its violence of sexual abuse against women of African descent and inhumane treatment of women lasted more than three centuries and continues to plague African Americans today.[32]

Racism

Consideration of racism in this study will focus on white supremacy and the violence it perpetrated and continues to perpetrate against black women and their identities. An example of this can be seen in the identities imposed on black women during and after slavery, compared with those imposed on white women. White women were generally seen as pure and ladylike, deserving of the utmost respect of all men, while women of African descent were the opposite. Womanist Diana Hayes examines the myth of womanhood as it relates to black and white women, and asserts that the myth demonstrated that a "black woman was all that a white woman should not be."[33] She draws on the story of Sojourner Truth, with her well-known statement: "Nobody ever helps me into carriages, or over mud-puddles, or gibs me de best places."[34] Truth then raises the question, "Ain't I a woman?" illustrating the difference in treatment by race. Finally, Hayes asserts that this racial dichotomy in gender understandings, which affirms white womanhood and negates black womanhood, will not dismantle the master's house until a

---

31. Healey, *Race, Ethnicity, Gender*, 112.
32. Healey, *Race, Ethnicity, Gender*, 112.
33. Hayes, "Feminist Theology," 326.
34. Truth, "Women's Rights," 57.

universal exploration of women is examined and the public sanctioning of the sins of racism and classism are investigated from a wider scope that is not white specific.[35] In other words, a study needs to be undertaken of the history of what society has deemed womanhood. The investigation into the concept of womanhood for black women will aid in the healing of their identity, help to restore their fractured self, and promote wholeness when society and the mainstream media, for example, begin to portray black women with the same respect and value as it portrays white women. Another example of the myth of womanhood and purity is explored by Jennifer Wriggins, an associate professor of law who investigates rape, racism, and the law. Wriggins illustrates how the inhumane treatment of black women was based on the color of their skin and the myth of black promiscuity.[36]

Roberts examines this notion as she explores the sexual abuse of enslaved women. She writes, "Jezebel defined black women in contradiction to the prevailing image of the true woman, who was virtuous, pure, and white."[37] She goes on to highlight an unidentified Southern white woman in 1904 saying, "I cannot imagine such a creature as a virtuous black woman."[38] As a consequence of this mindset, Roberts asserts the sexual exploitation of enslaved women became inevitable and necessary as a means to protect the virtuous purity of white women.[39] Lastly, the notion that white women possess purity suggests that black women are not pure and, thus, subjugates them to years of sexual violence by white and black men.

Danielle McGuire highlights this disparity in justice between black women and white women in *At the Dark End of The Street: Black Women, Rape and Resistance—A New History of the Civil Rights Movement from Rosa Parks to the Rise of Black Power*. In that book she explores the contrast in law, motivated by racial understandings, which protected white women while providing no justice for black women. As an example, McGuire describes the experience of Gertrude Perkins, a twenty-five-year-old African American woman who was raped by two police officers on her way home on March 27, 1949. They stopped her and forced her into the backseat of

---

35. Hayes, "Feminist Theology," 326–27.
36. Wriggins, "Rape, Racism, Law," 474.
37. Roberts, "Paradox Silence," 43.
38. Roberts, "Paradox Silence," 43.
39. Roberts, "Paradox Silence," 45.

the police car, then dragged her behind a building, where Perkins was repeatedly raped and assaulted by both officers at gunpoint.[40]

After two years of seeking justice, Perkins learned her accusers were found not guilty by an all-white, all-male jury. On the other hand, during that same time, white women often only had to speak of black men looking at them and the men were charged within the criminal justice system. For example, on June 4, 1951, a forty-one-year-old black farmer by the name of Mack Ingram was convicted of "eye rape" and received two years of hard labor because after an eighteen-year-old girl said he looked at her, even though Ingram was seventy-five feet away from the girl. The two examples show how black women were treated differently by the justice system due to assumptions about purity and impurity related to race.

Wriggins also highlights white supremacy and the violence towards black women as she explores rape and the injustice black women received within the law. She begins by highlighting rape through the nation's history, beginning with slavery until today. Wriggins asserts that black women where invisible and their experiences of forcible and coerced rape were not sensationalized nor publicized as were assaults of white women, nor was it seen as illegal. She states, "Harsh penalties [were] imposed on black offenders [for raping white women, however] . . . rape of black women by white or black men . . . was legal."[41]

West also examines the violence perpetrated against black women, sanctioned by notions of white supremacy. She argues that the function of violence was to devalue African American women as worthless and without dignity, and that the ideology of white supremacy imposed a forced silence on black women who were raped by black men. West asserts that this silence, which protected black men from the consequences of their own violence against black women, resulted from black women not wanting to participate in the racist systems of the dominant culture, which so frequently victimized black men. Thus, black women often internalized violence perpetrated against them by black males because they did not want to participate in the disrespecting and emasculation of black men by whites.[42]

Another practice sustained by racism was the use of black women as mammy—domestic help—to serve white men and women, and later black men. McElya's *Clinging to Mammy: The Faithful Slave in Twentieth-Century*

---

40. McGuire, *Dark End*, 53.
41. Wriggins, "Rape, Racism, Law," 468.
42. West, *Wounds Spirit*, 85, 183–84.

America emphasizes the color line and its effects on black women. McElya writes, "The problem of the color line, with its animating faithful slave narratives, has persisted into the twenty-first century. If we are to reckon honestly with the history and continued legacies of slavery in the United States, we must confront the terrible depths of desire for black mammy and the way it still drags at struggles for real democracy and social justice."[43] Collins also explores the stereotype of mammy and how it identified black women as nurturing "mammies," caring for other's children and neglecting their own.[44] In addition to identifying black women as promiscuous, they were also stereotyped as bad mothers—another effect of harmful and injurious identities stemming from the social construction of racism, sexism, and classism.[45]

Sheppard highlights the ramifications of racism on the psyches of black women, which overpowered any support received from religion, spirituality, and/or the black church. Seeking to deconstruct racist ideology, Sheppard points to the persistence of racism, and the need to explore its lasting psychic and cultural effects. Finally, the violent reality of racism can be seen as lives of black women and men continue to be negated by their senseless deaths by those who are charged to protect and serve. The need to have a Black Lives Matter movement and the cry for justice for the lives of black women and men as we mourn loss of life every twenty-eight minutes in the United States underscores that negation.[46]

The Black Lives Matter movement claims that "2014 was a year that saw profound injustice, and extraordinary resilience. Homicides at the hands of police sparked massive protests, meaning that America could no longer ignore bitter truths of the black experience. . . . This country must abandon the lie that the deep psychological wounds of slavery, racism and structural oppression are figments of the black imagination."[47]

Additionally, as the death toll rises from the black killings, the lack of justice, information, and media coverage of the killing of black women resounds with their invisibility and continues to negate them as the lowest in society. This is their lived reality, and we must be aware of that as they seek out counseling for their daily experience of oppression and violence.

---

43. McElya, *Clinging to Mammy*, 14.
44. Anderson et al., *Race, Class, Gender*, 81.
45. Anderson et al., *Race, Class, Gender*, 81.
46. Black Lives Matter, "Freedom & Justice."
47. Black Lives Matter, "Freedom & Justice."

In an online article by *The Huffington Post* this silence is highlighted as the "march for justice, the names of the women killed by police—particularly women of color killed by police—continues to be less known."[48] We need not forget their names: Tanisha Anderson, 37; Yvette Smith, 47; Miriam Carey, 34; Shelly Frey, 27; Darnisha Harris, 16; Malissa Williams, 30; Alesia Thomas, 35; Shantel Davis, 23; Rekia Boyd, 22; Shereese Francis, 29; Aiyana Stanley-Jones, 7; Tarika Wilson, 26; Kathryn Johnston, 92; Alberta Spruill, 57; Kendra James, 21; and Sandra Bland, 28.[49]

Listening and understanding is necessary in order to provide care for black women who may seek out treatment as they need safe spaces to explore their experiences of oppression, violence, grief, and injustice. *The Huffington Post* article illustrates this as the fight for justice continues for Kendra James's family ten years following her death, and still there is no justice. Moreover, four of the women named in *The Huffington Post* article were killed during police raids. Three of those women had children that were present when they were killed. Two of the women had mental illness and were killed as their family sought help. Instead of receiving aid for their sick loved one, they found themselves burying their daughters. Only one woman's death was vindicated, while seven of the killings resulted in no charges against the officers involved, and the cases remain open.[50]

Sexism

From the boarding of slave ships to landing in the Americas, African female slaves were forcibly raped by white men and later given to black slave men to create more property for the slave master.[51] Dwight Hopkins writes, "Formerly enslaved women remembered clearly the first form of sexual injustice. Mrs. Savilla Burrell reported Old Master was the daddy of some mulatto children. Other plantation owners segregated black women to use for sex. Any man could visit the segregated group to rape a black woman and then go about his business,"[52] because black women's bodies were used as objects for the sexual pleasure of white men and for the creation of wealth. Hopkins further illustrates this injustice toward enslaved

48. Abbey-Lambertz, "Black Women Killed."
49. Abbey-Lambertz, "Black Women Killed."
50. Abbey-Lambertz, "Black Women Killed."
51. Hopkins, "Enslaved Black Women," 292–94.
52. Hopkins, "Enslaved Black Women," 294.

African women when he states, "Beyond free access to black women's bodies and forced partnering, plantation owners also institutionalized breeding to create a future slave working force that was tall and strong. Breeders were enslaved women set aside to be impregnated by both white and black men in order to birth laborers at no cost to their owners."[53]

The stereotypical image of black women that emerged from the systemic sexist history of slavery can still be seen today as black women and girls struggle with their sexual identity—from Jezebel to Mammy. Therefore, I am highlighting a fractured self among black women which foster's the breaking of their mental, emotional, and spiritual selves as a result of inhumane treatment, dehumanization, oppression, objectification (sexual and non-sexual), and domestication. France Smith Foster points this fracture out as she explores the impact of stereotypes rooted in American slavery.[54] She describes the haunting effects of slavery as black women continue to view themselves as sexual or asexual beings—inherently immorally constructed versus inherently morally constructed. Moreover, she lifts up the importance of deconstruction, stating, "To lessen slavery's shadow over women and girls, we can begin with something as simple as understanding that some antebellum African American women were, and preferred to be addressed as, Ms./Mrs."[55] Foster's premise of understanding "Ms./Mrs." can aid in the deconstruction of the fractured self of black women and the heritage of slavery that restricted their identity to Mammy and Jezebel. Transitioning them from identities of asexual and immoral allows them to heal and become whole. Lastly, this viewpoint highlights how a womanist framework can create a safe and sacred space for black women to voice their experiences, receive affirmation, have an opportunity to deconstruct what has been used to tear them down, constructing a place where they are able to claim "Ms." or Mrs." as part of their identity.

Classism

The plight of black women, especially poor black women, can be seen in light of the economic injustices they continue to combat daily. Among other ramifications, slavery also created wealth and poverty. Hopkins explores the racial dichotomy in economic experience, focusing on ways in which black

---

53. Hopkins, "Enslaved Black Women," 291–94.
54. Foster, "Mammy's Daughters," 281.
55. Foster, "Mammy's Daughters," 281.

women (and black men) aided in the creation of wealth for white men and women for many generations, and the struggles of poor black women today. During slavery, black women were "the least of these," while white men, women, and their children were privileged based on their skin color and, sometimes, gender. The powers and principalities of culture saw white people, especially white men, as better, more acceptable, and more valuable on a cultural level, while blacks were dehumanized and interpreted as creatures whose only purpose was to serve the needs of the privileged. Black women worked in kitchens as cooks and domestics as they sewed, cleaned, cared for and maintained the master's home, and acted as maid to his wife and wet nurse to their children. They were used as breeders to create a free labor force, sexual objects for the gratification of white men, and field workers with black men. Their bodies and hands were used to create and maintain a system of wealth for plantation owners and society. Additionally, they had to tend to the needs of the slave community.

Even today, black women continue to be violated as they are subjected to the systemic violence of inequality. Hopkins writes, "After slavery, the United States government and individuals continued to foster the development of white wealth and to cripple the creation of black wealth. . . . This system of wealth differences began during the great suffering of the slave trade."[56] To demonstrate the disparity in poverty among blacks and whites, I will highlight the findings as reported by the "Dynamics of Economic Well-Being: Poverty, 2009–2011."[57] According to the report, blacks were 31 percent of the chronically poor, while whites were 2 percent.[58] The census report defined chronic poverty as "the percent in poverty every month of a given reference period. Chronic poverty over an annual period including individuals who have been in poverty for all twelve months, while chronic poverty refers to individuals in poverty all thirty-six months of the three-year period.[59]

A womanist understanding of class issues not only develops empathy toward the struggles of poor and working-class black women, it also moves beyond to explore the ethical implications created by the powers and principalities, and creates space for black women to give voice to their struggles as they engage Heinz Kohut's concept of empathy. With its framework of

---

56. Hopkins, "Enslaved Black Women," 297.
57. Edwards, "Dynamics Economic."
58. Edwards, "Dynamics Economic," 10, 32.
59. Edwards, "Dynamics Economic," 3.

listening and understanding, Kohut's concept is beneficial to the healing of black women.[60]

---

60. Kohut, *Analysis Cure*, 176.

2

Literature Review

Media, Literature, and the Images of Black Women

> Identity has to do with what one feels on the inside . . . [and] is the expression of one's self-understanding. . . . Rather, the person with a clear sense of identity always has a unifying self-concept that regulates the identity.
>
> —Lee H. Butler, *Liberating Our Dignity and Saving Our Souls*

THIS SECTION OF THE literature review explores images of black women in literature, movies, television, and music. I begin by highlighting ways in which *For Colored Girls Who Have Considered Suicide/When the Rainbow is Enuf* (*For Colored Girls*), *Beloved*, *The Color Purple*, and *12 Years A Slave* demonstrate my concept of the fractured self. Next, I explore stereotypes of black women as depicted in movies, television, and music, especially characters depicting black women as Jezebel and Mammy.

For Colored Girls is a choreopoem written by Ntozake Shange.[1] She uses words to paint a picture of the multigenerational experiences of black women, provide a glimpse into what it means to be black and female in American culture and how black women see themselves/how others see them, and explore influences on this self-identity. "Armored," a term coined by E.J. Bell and S.M. Nkoma,[2] describes an understanding of how black women are socialized. Armoring means to become a strong but still

---

1. Shange, *For Colored Girls*.
2. Bell et al., Our Separate Ways, 96.

nurturing black woman, taught to survive and adapt.³ This notion of armoring is relevant to my thesis as it illustrates how black women have been taught to cope with violence, and the oppression of racism, sexism and classism, in order to survive.

An instance of armoring is depicted in the movie *For Colored Girls*, directed by Tyler Perry and adapted from Shange's choreopoem. The example of armoring is illustrated by the character Crystal Wallace/Lady in Brown, played by actress Kimberly Elise. The Elise's character is a strong black woman who is in control of her emotions, married, employed, and a nurturing mother of two.⁴ Although she is in an abusive marriage,—her husband is an unemployed, alcoholic, war veteran suffering from post-traumatic shock syndrome and she is supporting the family emotionally and financially—her physical demeanor does not indicate anything is wrong. She is a woman who is doing what is necessary to survive and adapt, while her lived reality is one of oppression and abuse. Black girls, as they develop into black women, are socialized and instilled with cultural attitudes that denote two distinctions—being an African American and being a female, thus creating a "political strategy for self-protection" and assisting in "developing a psychological resistance to defy racism and sexism."⁵

In order to survive, black women have been taught to be resilient and to armor themselves. This practice and attitude, however, may have contributed to the development of a fractured self by not allowing black women to experience their pain and deal with acts of violence that have been perpetrated against them. Black women's experiences of violence have, indeed, made them resilient. However, this researcher wants to highlight the need for therapists to be culturally competent so that they can see beyond a woman's resiliency and engage black women's pain. Shange depicts this in her choreopoem as she describes the resilience of black women, including their desire to live and not die as a result of their experience—even when they considered suicide, but the rainbow was enuf.⁶

Resilience is an outcome of the stereotype of being depicted as ghouls, children of horror, the joke, animals and crazy.⁷ It is being tough, even while experiencing pain, loss, grief, and abuse. Sometimes it seems she can-

3. Wallace, "Womanist Legacy," 49.
4. Perry, *Colored Girls*.
5. Wallace, "Womanist Legacy," 49.
6. Shange, *For Colored Girls*, 17–19.
7. Shange, *For Colored Girls*, 17–19.

not hear anything—but maddening screams and the soft strains of death she cries to herself, as she still has to be the mother and wife, and support a family and raise grandchildren—caring, struggling, and faced with hard times.[8] Spirited is when she continues to long to know herself—sing her rhythms and her song of life.[9] She is strong even though she has been made to feel as though she has been dead so long.[10] The black women's fortitude is to continue on, even as she struggles to know the sound of her voice, to be seen as equal and beautiful, and find the freedom and power to claim her identity. Although black women possess the ability to be resilient, I argue that they need space to lament their hurts and learn other ways to cope besides compartmentalizing and even ignoring their pain. They need to allow themselves to be vulnerable.

Womanist Jacqueline Grant shapes this understanding of resilience by exploring the impact of racism, sexism, and classism, and the ways in which this concept of the "strong black woman"[11] can be interpreted as a means of survival, although she believes it has been misrepresented by others to deem black women as domineering, castrating matriarchs.[12] Wallace says the image of the strong black women is of one who can "continue to endure and withstand emotional pain."[13] Armoring and resiliency helped black women protect themselves in order to survive. And yet many developed fractured selves in the process because they were unable to deal with the insurmountable acts of violence perpetrated upon their minds, bodies, and souls. Exploring armoring and resiliency as components of black women's experience helps us to see how this mechanism needs to be explored within the therapeutic encounter.

Shange gives voice to the injustice, betrayal, and violence inflicted on black women for generations. She pronounces the feelings of invisibility, hopelessness, despair, heartbreak, and pain—the core and foundational reality of the black women's experience. Moreover, she asks questions that have been in the minds of black women for generations as she voices the concerns and thoughts of Lady in Brown[14]:

8. Shange, *For Colored Girls*, 17–19.
9. Shange, *For Colored Girls*, 17–19.
10. Shange, *For Colored Girls*, 17–19.
11. Walker-Barnes, *Too Heavy Yoke*, 14, 19.
12. Snorton, "African American Matriarch," 54.
13. Wallace, "Womanist Legacy," 47.
14. Shange, *For Colored Girls*, 17–19.

dark phases of womanhood
of never havin been a girl
half-notes scattered
without rhythm/no tune
distraught laughter fallin
over a black girl's shoulder. . .
don't tell nobody don't tell a soul. . .
lyrics/no voices. . .
are we ghouls?. . .
somebody/anybody. . .
sing a black girls song. . .
sing the song of her possibilities
sing a righteous gospel
let her be born
& handled warmly[15]

Shange's illustrates the need for a therapeutic modality that will make space for the unique experiences of black women, a therapeutic method that allows them to deconstruct negative depictions of their self-identities, to develop a sense of self-worth, and to be in a safe space that allows them to open up and become unarmored. They need to know that they are not ghouls, animals, horrors or jokes—but they are black women who have experienced violence and deserve to freely express their multiple-reality. According to Boyd-Franklin, "part of our internalized self-image is a result of *Maafa* and its wounding of the souls of African Americans during and after slavery, creating multigenerational consequences."[16] In summary, Lady in Brown expresses the lived reality of black women and implores black women and girls to sing their song. It supports the idea of the need for a therapeutic methodology that is (1) attentive to the history of violence that plagues the identities of black women and (2) provides a means for them to deconstruct their suffering, oppression, and be empowered in mind, body, and soul.

Toni Morrison's novel, *Beloved*, portrays the implications of a fragmented self by providing voice to Margaret Garner through the character of Sethe. Garner ran away to escape the confinement and cruelty of slavery

---

15. Shange, *For Colored Girls*, 17–19.
16. Boyd-Franklin, *Black Families*, 7.

in search of freedom.[17] When she was caught, she attempted to kill all of her children and then herself. However, only her baby girl died.[18] Three other children were injured. To understand what might lead a mother to kill her child, one must first reflect upon the lives of slave women and the lives they knew their children would endure as slaves. Freedom through death seemed better than the violence and oppression of slavery.[19] In this book, I explore the impact of violence on Sethe that led to her actions.

The internalization of slavery, white supremacy, racism, sexism, and patriarchy shaped Sethe's identity as property of the white slave master. She was used as a "breeder" and treated like an animal or any way the slave master deemed profitable. Morrison paints a vivid picture of Sethe's identity from the lens of her master, Schoolteacher. Morrison writes of Sethe, "She made fine ink, damn good soup, pressed collars . . . and had ten good years of breeding left . . . property that reproduced itself without cost.[20] Sethe was not only subjected to the whims of her master, but to those of the other white males on the plantation, as well. Schoolteacher's nephew violated Sethe during her pregnancy as he nursed on her breast. When she struggled against his advances, he beat her into submission.[21] Sethe was stripped of her humanity and objectified by her white master and other men. Schoolteacher's description of Sethe demonstrates his understanding of Sethe as a sexual being and domesticated object, existing only to provide him pleasure.

Morrison depicts the internalization of slavery's effects and its aftermath, showing how these became rooted in the mind, body, personhood, and self-identity of Sethe. She paints a vivid picture of the girl who ran, seeking freedom, safety, and security, but who was a woman living a life of isolation, loneliness, heartache, pain, and despair. Sethe's experience of the lack of empathy hindered her ability to develop a cohesive self. It was Sethe's experience of Sweet Home, the slave plantation where she lived, that drove her to run into the shed and kill her baby girl. Her dream of freedom, safety, and security died as she saw Schoolteacher, her master before she escaped from slavery, arrive at the wagon to claim his property—her and her children.

17. Morrison, *Beloved*, xvii.
18. Morrison, *Beloved*, xvii.
19. Morrison, *Beloved*, xvii.
20. Morrison, *Beloved*, 176–77, 269.
21. Morrison, *Beloved*, 176.

Morrison's powerful story exemplifies the effects of slavery, effects so tragic that a mother would show love to her child by killing it. Moreover, she shows how black women need freedom from victimization and the opportunity to develop coping skills to deal with their experience of violence. For Sethe, the only way to freedom for herself and her children was to kill them and herself, so that they could be with God.

Sethe's desire to be free from her history of violence raises the following questions that I believe are important to my research proposal as it relates to a model of care for black women: (1) What is freedom? (2) What does it mean to be free? (3) What is safety? and (4) How is safety obtained? Finally, there is the question regarding the relationship between Sethe and God—who for Sethe represents freedom, safety, and security. This points to the need for therapists to be aware of the significance and role of black women's faith and beliefs in the therapeutic setting. A recent study conducted by the American Association of Psychiatry highlights the role of religion and spirituality for African American women, noting it is more than a form of worship. It is community and support.[22]

Through Sethe's story, Morrison highlights the power of healing in community. It was the spirit of community when the women gathered together to pray outside in front of Sethe's home. It was the community of love and support that led Sethe and Beloved to open the door. Opening the door of the home signifies a new beginning for Sethe. As the women prayed of one accord, Sethe's old past was let go and her future was before her. This new future and transformation are signified in the release of butterflies that represent her past.

Monica Coleman asks, "How could an individual remember the terror of the bodily and psychic abuse of millions without suffering the kind of insanity Sethe [the protagonist] endured?"[23] Perhaps the solution is not exorcism but reconciliation of the past in community, holding one another together with the tar-like power of community building. The remembering in community created the space for healing for Sethe, and the reconciliation of communal relationships that were broken—creating security and safety for Sethe. The pain of her past is not forgotten. However, she no longer has to remember alone, but remembers in the sacredness and safety of community. She left Sweet Home with pain and suffering of loss, and it followed her. Now it has been released to create new memories and the space

22. Lim, *Cultural Psychiatry*, 418.
23. Coleman, *Making Way Out*.

to re-story her desire for a better home within a community reconciled back to her. Lastly, the remembering of the past in community was able to bring forth healing and re-construct the relationships that were broken, now unified in the strength of sisterhood.

Alice Walker's book, *The Color Purple*, tells the story of Celie who was dehumanized and violated sexually by her stepfather and husband.[24] She was forced to marry at a young age, impregnated by her stepfather twice, and bore the pain and sadness of seeing her babies taken from her and given away. Celie received virtually no love or compassion. Only her younger sister, Nettie, who was forced away by Celie's husband, Mr., loved her Celie. Celie's story is filled with hopelessness and despair. It depicts how her identity was fractured as a result of the lack of empathy, love, and compassion she experienced with her stepfather, husband, and community. After Celie's sister was forced away, there was no one to affirm her or provide her an opportunity to see herself as human. This is important as we explore the plight of black women and consider with them how healing may occur. From a womanist modality, healing can emerge when people deconstruct a negative identity that may be consumed with self-hate and internalize a new identity that is undergirded with self-love.

Healing for Celie, in this sense, can be seen in her relationship with Shug Avery. It was not until building a relationship with Shug, Mr.'s mistress, that Celie was able to mirror love. Shug represented a selfobject for Celie. It was in her relationship with Shug that Celie was able to internalize what she needed. Celie mirrored the love, warmth, and unconditional affirmation from Shug, thereby taking in what she needed and building upon her self-confidence and identity.[25]

In mirroring love, Celie was able to deconstruct the identity given to her by others as worthless, ugly, and created for men's sexual gratification, and gain her own voice and identity. As she gains her voice near the end of the book, which voice opens up a new identity for Celie, an identity not predicated upon her past but upon the love that she has learned to have for herself. This allowed her to re-story, to develop a new identity and sense of self-worth that were steps toward inner freedom. Finally, it enabled her to start a business, create community for herself, and reunite with her sister Nettie and her children.[26]

---

24. Walker, *Color Purple*.
25. Cooper-White, *Many Voices*, 110–11.
26. Spielberg, *Color Purple*.

LITERATURE REVIEW

12 Years A Slave is a narrative account of slave Solomon Northup.[27] The story describes Northrup's experience with Patsey, a twenty-three-year-old enslaved black woman. Patsey wanted to die because of the sexual violence she suffered at the hands of her master, and the dehumanization and abuse she encountered from her mistress, the master's wife.[28] Solomon, also known as Platt, describes the terror of one particular experience—a time when Patsey left the plantation on the Sabbath to travel to Mistress Harriett's plantation to get soap for bathing because Mistress Epps would not provide any soap, even though Patsey picked more cotton than any two men.[29]

When Patsey returned to the Epps plantation she was met with rage. Platt recalls being commanded by his master to whip Patsey, nearly to the point of death.[30] Although he did not want to, Platt had to comply or else receive the lashes. Platt paints a vivid picture of the gratification of the mistress as Patsey is stripped naked and tied down like an animal to be whipped, as well as how the master is not satisfied with the intensity of the whipping, although Platt has given Patsey at least thirty lashes and blood is flowing from her body. Instead of empathy, Patsey was visited with injustice, hatred, and wrath, and was subjected to sexual, emotional, and physical violence at the hands of her master and mistress.[31]

This is just one episode in Platt's vivid account of violence on the Epps plantation, violence that Patsey experienced in her mind, body, and soul. Platt also describes the master's sexual violations of Patsey and the mistress' jealousy and daily rants towards her. Each account highlights the significance and importance of the violence of the past experienced by the Patsey, but also the violence of today's "daughters of Patsey," whose own suffering has not been addressed.

In this account of violence towards Patsey, we see that she was used as the scapegoat for the anger held by Master Epps and the anger of Mistress Epps. Cheryl Kirk-Duggan explores this scapegoating. Patsey is desired by her master and evokes jealousy of her mistress. She becomes the buffer—the master desires her sexually and has control over her, while the mistress desires to see her punished for being desired by her husband, and so the rivalry of violence begins. When the master cannot find her, Patsey is punished. And

---

27. Northup, *12 Years*.
28. Northup, *12 Years*, 254, 259.
29. Northup, *12 Years*, 255.
30. Northup, *12 Years*, 255–56.
31. Northup, *12 Years*, 255–57.

because the master wants her, she is punished by the mistress. Kirk-Duggan writes, "The scapegoat is the buffer when two or more have competing desire for the same object and that intense desire leads to envy, followed by rivalry, then violence. But violence against a scapegoat breaks down differences and makes competing humans more alike."[32]

The sexual exploitation of black women continues to be heard and seen in rap music and videos. This points to ways in which the stereotype of Jezebel, that began in slavery, continues to infect younger generations of black women and contribute to a fractured self that has internalized negative self-images. By using the recording industry and the airwaves, black and white boys and men in the rap industry inflict violence upon black women by depicting them as sexual objects. This is yet another form of sexism in today's society.

"Face Down," by rap artists Meek Mill and Trey Songz, depicts and degrades women as sexual objects for the pleasure of men. In the video, a man spanks a black female with money while she gyrates from a pole, barely dressed. The song's lyrics deny her humanity and identify her a whore.[33]

This dehumanization, and sexual exploitation in media such as this, raises many questions, including one of who promotes this image. In other words, who has the money and power to continue the legacy of violence against the identity of black women? And, finally, does the black woman's body today remain a product to be profited from and who profits? Roberts asserts that today, black women are not only objectified and profited from, but the construct of gender inequality between black men and women is reinforced.[34] The sexual subject matter, objectification, and stereotypes are then internalized by society and reinforce a fractured self of black women.

Furthermore, as we explore images of black women in television, we continue to find the role identities of Jezebel and Mammy. On the television show "Scandal," for instance, leading lady Olivia Pope—although a powerful black woman—is portrayed as Jezebel. She is sleeping with a white married man, who happens to be the president of the United States. This also depicts issues of power that will be explored later in the book.

Another recent television drama depicts both Jezebel and Mammy identities for black women. In "The Have's and the Have Not's," one woman, in order to gain access to what whites possess, prostitutes herself by sleeping with

---

32. Kirk-Duggan, *Misbegotten Anguish*, 45.
33. Meek Mill, "Face Down."
34. Roberts, "Paradox Silence," 47.

a white married man, while another is a "Mammy," who cleans and works as a domestic for a prominent white family. While the African American writers of these popular shows are obviously talented, their work continues to perpetuate unhealthy stereotypes about black women. Through the depictions of "Scandal" and "The Have's and the Have Not's," we are able to see stereotypes of black women as oversexed, promiscuous women.[35]

In conclusion, in an article exploring sexual stereotypes depicted in rap videos, Shani Peterson describes a study of young black girls from low-income, high-crime neighborhoods who listened to rap. He found that among girls who watched rap videos with exploitative images of women, many used drugs and alcohol, had multiple sex partners, and experienced low self-esteem.[36] Peterson's study points to ways in which black girls continue to be affected by stereotypes derivative of the long history of sexual violence stemming from enslavement, and demonstrates that this harms their mental and physical health, and creates a fractured self.

Investigation of the Need for Adequate Theoretical Approaches for African American Women

In "Mammy's Daughters; Or the DNA of a Feminist Sexual Ethics," Foster writes, "The identities imposed upon us shape how we see ourselves, and how we see others."[37] Foster illustrates how negative stereotypes may create fragmented identities within black women, and how externalizing negative stereotypes introduces new ways to identify self, allowing them to examine their history and adopt an ethical view of self that is healing and life giving, in contrast to dehumanizing and immoral. Sheppard explores the impact on self as black women struggle with their bodies and skin color, and as their images are portrayed negatively within culture, community, and even in their own families. Because black women's relationships to their bodies result from early American history constructed in slavery, Sheppard asserts that the survival and liberation of black women rests on the ability to deconstruct negative experiences.[38]

Deconstruction will allow black women to repair self-deficits such that they can move toward what psychoanalytic thinker Kohut describes a

---

35. Anderson et al., *Race, Class, Gender*, 81.
36. Peterson, "Images Sexual Stereotypes," 1157–64.
37. Foster, "Mammy's Daughters," 280.
38. Sheppard, *Self, Culture*, 151.

"continuity of self."[39] Sheppard, for instance, explores the need for a womanist-informed self psychology as it re-centers the importance of making specific inquiries and is aware of the broader cultural dynamics for black women and the development of their psyches.[40] Similarly, Butler writes, "Through the rise of the 'self,' the individual becomes free . . . becoming new creatures in the likeness of the Son as one is restored to community."[41] These perspectives point to the self, and allude to its fragmentation and consider how its exploration can lead to healing from fragmentation. These resources, as well as others provided in this research project, illustrate the need for particular theoretical approaches for African American women that speak to their multiple-reality experience.

Casey T. Taft, Thema Byrant-Davis, Halley E. Woodward, Shaquita Tillman, and Sanda Tores explore violence towards African Americans and the need for further research to better serve and address the needs, experiences, and mental health of African American women.[42] Black women experience violence, including intimate partner violence and its consequences, at higher rates than do white women. Despite this fact, there is little literature available to address cultural and structural factors relevant to the mental health and physical safety of African American women.[43]

According to the authors of a recent article exploring intimate partner violence among African American women, this points to the fact that black women have been neglected in white society by one-size-fits-all methods and theoretical approaches to the epidemic of violence:

> There is a concern that the one-size-fits-all approach to theory and intervention does not capture the unique experience of African Americans. . . . In some African American communities there is limited access to . . . transportation, employment, opportunities, affordable medical care, social and mental health services, homeless and domestic shelters, police protection, and legal services. . . . Issues related to racism, discrimination, and mistreatment by service providers demean those seeking assistance, resulting in a lack of utilization of services offered to African American victims.[44]

---

39. Sheppard, *Self, Culture*, 116.
40. Sheppard, *Self, Culture*, 119–20.
41. Butler, *Liberating Our Dignity*, 99.
42. Taft et al., "Intimate Partner Violence," 50.
43. Taft et al., "Intimate Partner Violence," 51.
44. Taft et al., "Intimate Partner Violence," 50–51.

The authors point out that violence against black women happens in all socio-economic contexts, not just among those who are poor and/or uneducated. The authors offer multiple examples of experiences with violence and its consequences to unfold the story and to point to the implications of a lack of resources for helping. They also challenge the uniform treatment approach and argue for culturally competent training, including exploration of racial and socio-economic oppression, for persons in positions to provide care for African American women who are victims of violence (i.e., counselors, shelter staff, etc.).[45]

"Recommendations for the Psychological Treatment of Persons of African Descent," written by black psychologists Linda Myers, Anthony Young, Ezemenari Obasi, and Suzette Speight, highlights the importance of strengthening a cultural ethos that represents a holistic and inclusive framework grounded in one's history, as opposed to a mono-cultural hegemonic Western perspective.[46] To make their point the psychologists begin by exploring diagnostic assessment and pathology as defined within a Western construct, pointing to how it may misdiagnose persons of African descent. Myers, Young, Obasi, and Speight survey how the Western diagnostic assessment is deficient as it lacks a holistic and integrative approach with cultural dimension. Lifting up the fact that traditional psychological models arising from a Western paradigm may be more rigid and individualistic, they write:

> A consequence . . . of mental health [due to their lacking an African worldview] have not been inclusive of the more holistic and integrative definitions that require focus on the society/community and the individual moral and economic development, respect for nature and humanity, the spiritual and material aspects of being . . . the notion of communalism is often replaced by an individualistic . . . mode of interaction.[47]

Furthermore, the authors argue that Western orientations focus primarily on pathology, on an individual level, without attending to a cultural worldview that recognizes societal functions and relationships. This broader view provides a multi-dimensional perspective when working with persons of African descent. "Embracing mental health as a multi-dimensional construct concerned with the entire community, past and

---

45. Taft et al., "Intimate Partner Violence," 55, 57.
46. Myers et al., "Recommendations Psychological Treatment," 13.
47. Myers et al., "Recommendations Psychological Treatment," 13–15.

future generations, and the physical environment, a range of psychological issues from mental illness to the problems of daily life, would all have to be potential targets for intervention."[48]

Implementing a cultural perspective and acknowledging the history of oppression and dehumanization experienced by persons of African descent may decrease the frequent misdiagnosis that places them as having a higher rate of severe mental illnesses, according to the authors and their research. The authors recognize that misdiagnosis may result from the therapist's misrepresentation of the counselee, and the history of social biases that constructed negative images and stereotypes of persons of African descent. The authors write:

> The approximation of quality treatment and service delivery will therefore require helping professionals to look at themselves and gain the level of self-knowledge in which one's biases resulting from socialization in this [Western] culture are acknowledged, and monitored throughout the process of engagement, diagnosis and treatment.... It is imperative... that stereotypes and images [of persons of African descent] be integrated for self-serving bias and set aside [before working with them], or refer them to a more competent professional.[49]

Myers, Young, Obasi, and Speight engage the reader with the importance of being aware of present biases, and how biases may hinder making an accurate diagnosis when working with people of African descent, arguing that the dominant group may even consider one to be "insane," based on a hegemonic Western mono-cultural construct. For instance, the diagnostic term "drapetomania" was created in the 1800s as a term for trying to escape from one's abuser.[50] They discuss the need for a therapeutic modality that is aware of the multidimensional reality of black women and allows the counselee and the therapist to externalize negative stereotypes that have been internalized as they grew out of the history of oppression and were supported by violence of many types.

In conclusion, Myers, et al., present a holistic and integrative therapeutic modality that speaks to the need for competent therapists who are culturally aware of and who acknowledge the particular history of persons of African descent so that healing can occur. Furthermore, they argue for

---

48. Myers et al., "Recommendations Psychological Treatment," 13.
49. Myers et al., "Recommendations Psychological Treatment," 14.
50. Myers et al., "Recommendations Psychological Treatment," 14.

moving away from an individualistic modality and embracing a communal framework that is inclusive and aware of the entire person in his or her context. This holistic, integrative approach benefits both the individual and community. It can heal the fragmented selves of black women and permit the wholeness described by McCrary—a balance of mind, body, and soul— to be achieved.

Richie highlights the need for the exploration of violence in the context of the lives of poor black women. Moreover, Richie highlights the journey of the anti-violence movement, damage to black women as a result of their experience of violence, and the lack of a voice to speak against violence within their contexts. Richie argues for a black feminist modality to explore the violence that afflicts black women who are negated as a result of racism, sexism, and classism. Richie's depiction of violence toward black women is paralleled by the injustice of their imprisonment. Her premise lifts up the systemic issues that continue to re-victimize black women by locking them up without considering the violence and other life experiences that caused them to be deemed as criminals.

Further, Richie provides a theoretical argument to end violence against black women by implementing what she describes as "the male violence matrix"[51] that analyzes male violence toward black women utilizing a black feminist framework focused on gender subordination, structural racism, class inequality, genderism, and other injustices that do not adequately address the needs of black women who suffer from violence.[52] While Richie focuses on ending violence experienced by poor African American women, she does not offer a framework for a therapeutic modality that educates the therapist to engage the narratives of African American women who experience violence and are searching for a safe space for healing. Taft, et al., examine the need for a therapeutic modality concerned with the impact of violence experienced by black women but do not provide a modality that heals the epidemic of violence experienced by them. However, they do initiate a dialogue about the importance and urgency of this.

Roberts in "Paradox of Silence" and Emilie Townes in "From Mammy to Welfare Queen: Images of Black Women in Public Policy Formation" both provide a look into the implications of slavery, the impact of slavery, and the role of religion during slavery.[53] They also explore slavery's impact

---

51. Richie, *Arrested Justice*, 127.
52. Richie, *Arrested Justice*, 160.
53. Townes, "From Mammy," 66.

on social values, religious thought, and the truth regarding economics. Roberts explores the implications of slavery, including sexual violation of black slave women and girls and the stereotypes derived from this. Townes explores the brutalizing images of black womanhood and the correlation between their identity and slavery. Both Roberts and Townes highlight the effect of slavery on the image of black women for the women, themselves, and society at large. Further, each engages the readers with the importance of acknowledging and understanding slavery and the formation of black women as non-human. Roberts and Townes speak to the importance of recognizing the systemic oppression, dehumanization, and objectification experienced by black women today.

McCrary provides a framework for my understanding of the fragmentation of African American women created within a system of oppression. She illustrates the detriment that occurs within women who have been violated by a system of oppression and violence that leads to brokenness and the need for wholeness. Her work speaks to the ability to become whole, and the healing that occurs within the same. McCrary's work also suggests that the wholeness that occurs within women who have experienced violence brings healing and restoration in the relationships they hold.

My goal is to acknowledge the unique, multidimensional reality of black women and highlight the role of that multidimensional reality in the development of self in relationships with self, community, and God. This viewpoint postulates becoming whole requires rejecting weakness and claiming a healthy understanding of self.

3

Theoretical and Theological Framework

> Making a way out of no way involves God's presentation of unforeseen possibilities; human agency; the goal of justice, survival. And quality of life; and a challenge to the existing order.... The activity of healing ... is the actively restoring wholeness and community where there is exclusion, corruption, individualism, fragmentation, and brokenness.
>
> —Monica A. Coleman, *Ain't I a Womanist, Too?*

As stated previously, the main research question for this study is: What injurious and harmful values based in slavery (dehumanization, domestication, racism/white supremacy, classism, and sexism) have been internalized by African American women and fostered the creation of a fractured self? Also essential to this study are these sub-questions:

1. How do (some) black women become fragmented?
2. How does this fragmentation hinder them in the world and impact their ability to build healthy relationships and a healthy self-identity?
3. What external factors in their lived reality foster this fragmented (identification of) self?

The integration of theoretical concepts from womanist, self psychology, and African-centered psychology allow me to convey a method that I describe as "midwifing." Midwifing is a concept that provides guidance, affirmation, compassionate care, and support for black women. It fosters empowerment and liberation, allowing women to connect with self, community, and God. Midwifing is aware of the impact that one's culture and socialization has on the development of the structure of self. I believe this method will aid in revealing the negative identities of black women, and move them from a fragmented self to a cohesive self.

Midwifing is an effective method of moving black women from a fragmented to cohesive self because it (1) establishes a safe therapeutic space that allows black women to construct a therapeutic alliance, (2) postulates a position of empathy allowing them to feel free to open up and explore their defense mechanisms, (3) allows black women to experience the therapist as affirming and understanding, (4) recognizes their humanity, (5) enables black women to become empowered and liberated in order to deconstruct negative identification, and (6) develops a healthy core self and relationship with the community, and allows black women to see themselves in the image of God as they develop a mature self through repairing self-deficits. Lastly, healing, transformation, and wholeness become possible as the counselor, utilizing midwifing, creates the space for the thick experience of black women to be heard.[1] Midwifing allows the counselor to gain insight and understanding of the experience of some black women, thereby holding and providing support for black women to explore their true experience, then move them to a place where they are able to thrive and integrate all the parts of their experience so that they can become a cohesive self.

Womanist Theoretical Framework

A womanist framework values the importance and uniqueness of the multiple reality experience of black women and serves as a conduit to empower and journey with black women, to enabling them to cultivate their own true identity separate from what has been imposed on them via socialization, miseducation, and other external forces. The framework begins with and values the experience of black women. Further, it seeks to create a safe space that allows black women to become unarmored, thus helping to un-armor defensive and protective mechanisms by being aware of black women's multiple reality experience and internalization of the matriarch (strong black woman) image. Internalization of the matriarchal image is explored later in this chapter.

The womanist theoretical framework was birthed to give voice to women of color and their unique experiences within their contexts. Womanist theologian, pastor, and author MarKeva Gwendolyn Hill asserts that, "Womanism was born out of the exclusion and misinterpretation of

---

1. Cooper-White, *Braided Selves*.

women of color . . . [lifting up] Patricia Hill Collins's conjecture that [white feminists] . . . failed to challenge controlling images such as mammy."[2] Womanist theory explores and deconstructs oppression perpetrated against women of color and their unique experiences. Their tri-dimensional experiences of racism, sexism, and classism are all forms of violence that have plagued the minds, bodies, and souls of black women, which is explored later in the book.

Womanist theory dialogues with culture, socialization (including the effects of patriarchy), male dominance, white supremacy, and spiritual, religious, and/or theological beliefs, past and present (including during slavery). It expresses concern for the entire family, and seeks to nurture black women in the process of developing healthy self-images and healthy relationships. This platform makes possible the exploration of injurious and harmful values based in slavery that have been internalized by African American women and that may have fostered a fractured self. It also provides a model of care that embraces black women's multiple life experiences in response. Through attention to the fractured selves of African American women and the deconstruction of negative stereotypes, womanist theory provides voice, empowerment, and liberation to black women. Its framework undergirds black women and helps them re-define what it means to be a strong black women by providing healing and healthy ways to process, cope, and exist, as it honors and acknowledges their multiple reality experience.

As noted in the introduction, the term womanism was coined in 1982 by African American author and activist Alice Walker.[3] In this book, I draw on Delores Williams's definition of womanism. Williams declares:

> Womanist theology is a prophetic voice concerned about the well-being of the entire African American community, male and female, adults, and children. Womanist theology attempts to help black women see, affirm, and have confidence in the importance of their experience and faith in the African American community. Womanist theology challenges all oppressive forces impeding black women's struggle for survival and for the development of a positive, productive quality of life conducive to women's and the family's freedom and well-being. Womanist theology opposes all oppression based on race, sex, class, sexual preference, physical ability, and caste.[4]

2. Hill, *Womanism Against Socially*, 63.
3. Walker, *Search Mothers Gardens*.
4. Williams, *Sisters Wilderness*, 67.

Womanist scholar and pastoral theologian Crumpton highlights that a womanist paradigm shifts away from the dominant culture, thereby creating spaces that allow for the experience of black women to be heard and deems their story significant and important.[5]

Lastly, a womanist methodology explores and acknowledges the experiences of African American women past and present as it reflects, validates, and honors the lives and contributions of their enslaved ancestors. Moreover, it helps these women to see themselves in God's image and allows them to interweave their religious and/or spiritual beliefs into the therapeutic encounter, thus affirming their past, culture, heritage, blackness, womanhood, and faith. It elaborates, validates, and acknowledges their resourcefulness, innate strength, and contributions to the sustaining and creating of life, family, and community. A womanist framework provides a holistic, healing approach as it creates space for black women to share, hear, and acknowledge their stories—which in turn helps them to affirm a stronger self-identity as they embrace their humanity and begin to integrate their experiences, moving from fractured selves to wholeness.

A womanist framework includes the pastoral functions of nurturing, empowering, liberating, and reconciling. This can be a therapeutic means for wholeness, healing, and transformation in the lives of black women, and can lead to a watering of self that externalizes a fragmented identity. Womanist pastoral theologian Ali's approach sufficiently explores the objectives of my theological methodology as she focuses on how each component of the womanist framework aids in the healing and transformation of black women, moving them from a fractured self to becoming whole and healthy as they are met with an approach that allows them to become un-armored and embrace their humanness. Additionally, Ali's approach resonates with my theological anthropology. She affirms that (1) persons are free to exist in society, (2) persons are invited to be in relationship with God and the community, and (3) persons are visible to self/others and empowered to value self as created in the image of God. In other words, a healthy theological anthropology affirms all people, freeing them to participate in/develop relationships with God and other human beings. No one is excluded or harmed due to differences such as race, gender, religion/faith beliefs, sexual orientation, class, and/or ability. Moreover, this anthropology embraces the "other," deems them visible, and moves them from a place of marginality to inclusivity.

5. Crumpton, *Crafting*, 39.

In particular, theological anthropology seeks to bring African American women into relationship with God, as well as allow them to claim their identity through God's lens. This understanding provides a theoretical framework to challenge the fractured selves of black women resulting from negative messages (received via media and other forms of oppression) that then often are adopted in the psyches of young black women. Additionally, Ali's method integrates black theology (black liberation theology and womanist theology), black literature/philosophy, and African-centered psychology, which speak to the multidimensional experience of African American women in the United States today.

Ali's work explores the importance of the black experience within the framework of pastoral theology as she broadens what was theorized by Seward Hiltner, one of the founding fathers of the modern discipline of pastoral theology.[6] Ali adds to Hiltner's contribution as she brings in the voice and plight of poor black women (and their children) and their status within the United States at the bottom of the social, political, and economic spectrum. Overall, Ali's framework exposes the oppressive forces that impact the experience of African women (and men), and explores African American women's unique tri-dimensional experience of racism, classism, and sexism within Western society.

Ali argues that what needs to be addressed from a pastoral perspective is "the communal need for survival and liberation that (1) begins with the experience of the culture verses objectifications and abstractions about culture, (2) allows for the significance of communality verses individuality, and (3) expands the operations of ministry."[7] She begins by re-defining pastoral theology in the African American context as "a theological reflection on the experience of the cultural context as relevant for strategic pastoral care giving in the context of ministry."[8] Thus, she affirms the importance of beginning with the experience that is indigenous to the cultural context and creating a two-step process that places the counselee/parishioner experience ahead of that of the pastoral caregiver. Further, Ali declares, "An awareness of the subjective experience of the cultural context is necessary to modify and/or correct the objective experience of the pastoral caregiver. The communal concern for the majority of African Americans requires a community effort or a network of caregivers working with the pastor/

---

6. Watkins Ali, *Survival Liberation*, 10.
7. Watkins Ali, *Survival Liberation*, 8.
8. Watkins Ali, *Survival Liberation*, 11.

pastoral caregiver; and pastoral care needs of the African American context require . . . *nurturing, empowering, liberating* and *reconciling.*"[9]

Ali describes "nurturing" as care that is consistent and enables one to gain strength in the midst of struggle. Through nurturing, the pastoral care giver seeks to respond to human need(s) by understanding and providing care for the duration that is needed in order to be supportive and hold persons within and throughout the crisis moment. "Empowering" positions people to get in touch with their own power, which allows them to resist oppression and gain control of their life. By means of empowering, one is able to claim one's voice and experience, which often have been stolen, and to recover one's self. This allows persons to move forward from stagnation to growth.

"Liberating" requires action in the pastoral care moment that frees persons spiritually and politically from oppressive forces and systems that have burdened them with internalized negative identifications. This, in turn, frees persons to speak to and deconstruct oppressive structures. "Reconciling" is the "act of reclaiming, restoring, and retaining African American philosophy and culture in ministry to African Americans."[10] As a result of reconciling, African Americans will begin to reconcile themselves with one another, lost traditions, heritage, community, and a different class status, thus reducing and/or eliminating fratricide among young boys. Ali's perspective illustrates a communal approach for providing care within an African American context by way of nurturing, empowering, liberating, and reconciling.

Ali understands nurturing, empowering, liberating, and reconciling combats oppression. This allows black women to see themselves in the image of God, and illustrates a God that is on the side of the oppressed. My perspective on the importance of a theological anthropology that seeks to free black women from oppressive forces and journey with them as they claim a God who is on the side of the oppressed is deeply influenced by Ali's perspective. This perspective empowers black women to become visible through the care provider's work of healing, sustaining, guiding, nurturing, empowering, liberating, and reconciling, so that the women might embrace their humanity. In summary, Ali's framework helps women to move from a fractured state to achieving external and internal wholeness through self-exploration and understanding of self, God, and community.

9. Watkins Ali, *Survival Liberation*, 8–9.
10. Watkins Ali, *Survival Liberation*, 121.

Self-Psychology

Kohut's self-psychology offers potential for healing for black women as he considers the effects of negative cultural, environmental, and external forces that play a role in the fragmentation of the self, especially in his focus on faulty selfobjects. Although Kohut does not specifically speak to the experience of black women, his exploration of the impact of unmet needs on the self speaks to the plight of African American women in the development of their self-esteem and identity.[11] This book seeks to highlight some of Kohut's concepts such as empathy, self, selfobject, optimal frustration, mirror transference, idealizing transference, cohesive self, twinship/alter ego transference, and transmuting internalization.[12] However, the primary focus is on the benefits of empathy and transmuting internalization for strengthening the self of the black woman to move her from a fragmented (fractured self) to a cohesive self (wholeness). Therefore, self-psychology creates a theoretical framework that stimulates emotional progression within black women who have developed an unhealthy self as a result of unmet needs.

Kohut's framework is shaped by his interpretation of narcissistic disorder, which he believes results from the lack of idealizing and mirroring in the parent-/caregiver-child relationship. He explores interpersonal relationships between child and caregivers in order to clarify self-development. For example, he argues that a parent's ability or inability to respond empathically to the child plays a role in the development of the child's identity and self-esteem. Therefore, it is the failure of the child's early selfobjects that creates an unhealthy self and leads the child to promote an unhealthy grandiose self. Kohut formulates an interpretation of pathology stemming from the child's unmet needs during the parent/child dyad relationship, which keeps the child from developing a healthy self-esteem.

Kohut emphasizes that for healthy development, a child needs to receive proper mirroring from the selfobject.[13] This helps the child to develop self-confidence and basic self-esteem, at least some of the time. Moreover, Kohut believes that the development of one's self is a continuing process that occurs over the duration of one's life. Thus, with its emphasis on empathy and introspection, the Kohutian therapeutic approach is valuable when

---

11. Crumpton, *Womanist Pastoral Theology*.
12. Kohut, *Analysis Cure*, 4, 98–110, 174–75, 192–94.
13. Kohut, *Restoration*.

working with black women. Kohut believes that empathy and introspection should be used as tools in psychoanalysis to study human experience and the core self of the client. His interpretation of empathy is "not that of niceness . . . [but] 'vicarious introspection.'"[14]

Empathy is valuable in counseling African American women because the empathic approach emphasizes contextual human understanding rather than technical competence. This highlights the importance of presenting patience and understanding as black women seek to share their experiences from their own perspectives. Sincere efforts at understanding facilitate the creation of a space that allows black women to share more deeply. Thus, the pastoral counselor can "walk in their shoes" and provide interpretation that coincides with their experience, rather than simply pathologizing their perspectives.

The goal of therapy, therefore, is not to be right but to listen and practice understanding. Moreover, Kohut's therapeutic goal helps to strengthen self-deficits of black women who may be fractured via what he calls optimal frustration, which leads black women to experience transmuting internalization, allowing for the development of a mature selfobject. Kohut's method creates an opportunity to examine oppressive and harmful experiences internalized by African American women, and helps them move from an unhealthy (fractured) self to a self that is healthy and able to move forward in life—not just existing, but embracing life and all that life have to offer (wholeness). Kohut asserts, "The analysts will even have to realize that a patient whose childhood selfobjects failed traumatically in this area will require long periods of 'only' understanding."[15]

This two-fold framework of empathy and introspection allows the therapist to listen, and provides black women with the space needed to get out and express conscious and unconscious feelings and thoughts about themselves. Additionally, the clinical data gathered as a result of listening and observation allow the counselor to acknowledge black womens' experiences, listen with empathy (listening to her experience from her perspective), and pay attention to their context—background, circumstances, socialization, environment—so that the therapist can avoid letting his/her own experiences interfere with hearing the multidimensional reality of

---

14. Kohut, *Analysis Cure*, 175.
15. Kohut, *Restoration*, 88.

black women.[16] Again, this allows women to be heard and to move from a fragmented to a cohesive identity.

Self-psychology, as articulated by Kohut, aims at the importance of the client/patient becoming a whole nuclear self by being able to witness idealized mirroring. Kohut writes, "What creates the matrix for the healthy development of a healthy self in the child is the selfobject's capacity to respond with proper mirroring at least some of the time."[17] The role of the therapist is to utilize transference that allows the client/patient to become a healthy core self within or as a result of the therapeutic encounter. Kohut named his ultimate goal of therapy as being the development of a healthy and balanced self, which he called a "cohesive self."

Kohut speaks of the cohesive self as a psychic structure that becomes harmonious, vigorous, and energetic. In other words, it is an integrated self that is able to develop a structured/organized self.[18] To develop a cohesive self, Kohut argues, the child/client needs to experience what he describes as "optimal frustration."[19]

Kohut examines optimal frustration as resulting from the non-responsiveness or discrepancy of the selfobject—the withdrawal of the mirroring selfobject repeats the traumatic unavailability of self-conforming responses in early life or, in a case of structural neurosis, the analyst's absence is experienced as a repetition of the primal scene . . . and 'transmuting internalization'—a result of transference in the therapeutic relationship that leads to replacement of the selfobjects—fills the defect of the self.[20]

Optimal frustration within the therapeutic space allows the client to strengthen his/her self and facilitates transmuting internalization (the process by which a function previously performed by another is taken into the self and made one's own). This allows a mature selfobject to emerge. In conclusion, Kohut's therapeutic technique of empathic attunement creates an opportunity for the client to repair the break that occurred from the childhood selfobject, to develop healthy narcissism, and to nurture new relationships with new selfobjects. The consistency of the therapist's empathic attunement liberates black women from enforced silence about the

---

16. Kohut, *Restoration*, 145.
17. Kohut, *Restoration*, 188.
18. Kohut, *Analysis Cure*, 99–100.
19. Kohut, *Analysis Cure*, 99–103.
20. Kohut, *Analysis Cure*, 99–103.

harm they have experienced. This empowers them to voice and examine their experiences, thus sanctioning a healthy self-identity for them.

African-Centered Psychological Method

African-centered psychology is a holistic modality that is inclusive and culturally aware of African Americans and their diverse, rich history beginning in Africa and continuing with descendants scattered across the globe. The methodology attends to the fact that African Americans had a history and existence before being enslaved. Moreover, it attempts to reclaim a history for black women before the voyage to America and their dehumanizing experience of tri-dimensional oppressive violence in racism, sexism, and classism. This consciousness of African Americans' formation and development of self and related cultural implications are important when working with persons of African descent in the United States because it allows the therapist to journey with those persons as they reclaim their humanness and become un-armored.

An African-centered approach affirms African descendants' way of being in an anti-African environment.[21] It is aware of the daily life experiences of systemic, institutional, and other forms of oppression encountered by persons of African descent. Likewise, this modality embraces and is aware of African American spiritualities, as well as African Americans experiences of oppression, dehumanization, and exploitation in the United States. In *Rooted in the Earth: Reclaiming the African Environmental Heritage*, historian and environmentalist Diane Glave illustrates the connection between racism/exploitation and the land, showing, for example, how whites used the agricultural knowledge of the enslaved to help them develop a system of wealth while the enslaved were victims of racism and socioeconomic oppression during and after slavery.[22] Glave writes, "Racism fueled Southern monoculture and agriculture, giving legitimacy to slaveholders' exploitation of the skills and labor of the enslaved, who rapidly and extensively redefined the Southern landscape."[23]

Components within the African-centered methodology I focus on are culture, spirituality, collectivism, oral tradition/history, and *sankofa*. Each component lifts up the importance of culture and worldview in considering

21. Myers et al., "Recommendations Psychological Treatment," 15.
22. Glave, *Rooted Earth*, 9.
23. Glave, *Rooted Earth*, 9.

the shaping of the self. Moreover, each assists in the deconstruction of the black woman's fractured self. Utilizing an African-centered method allows black women to become authentically human outside of a Western ideology of what is and is not beautiful. Additionally, it creates an opportunity for black women to move beyond merely surviving as existence to surviving and living into the women they were created to be, without the stigma of becoming or existing as others have defined them. This allows them to become unarmored, externalize injurious and harmful values based in slavery that aided in a fragmented self, and move to a cohesive self that is strengthened, developing a structure that is strong and organized. Lastly, it allows them to build healthy relationships and a healthy self-identity.

Meyers, et al., hypothesize that in order for African Americans to be helped by clinicians, the clinicians' Western orientation needs to be addressed and explored. Only in this way can they provide a healthy and careful evaluation and assessment of African Americans who seek care. Additionally, they name the need to approach the client from a historical understanding that reflects their diverse cultural history and background.[24] Na'im Akbar asserts that a black perspective redefines the perception that blacks are inferior and offers a viewpoint that is proactive as opposed to reactive.[25] Similarly, Joseph L. White asserts, "It is difficult, if not impossible, to understand the lifestyles of Black people using traditional theories developed by White psychologists to explain White people. Moreover, when these traditional theories are applied to the lives of Black folk, many incorrect, weakness-dominated, and inferiority-oriented conclusions come about, as highlighted by Belgrane and Allison."[26]

Psychologist Linda Myers writes, "We as a people experienced the psychology of oppression, and it is the sub-optimal worldview that is oppressive. We have been led to believe that our very physical survival was in the hands of another man; we have been denied access to the truth about our cultural heritage and story; our cultural heritage and history have been negated, and that of sub-optimal thinkers elevated."[27] This perspective allows black women to be connected with an African-centered culture, her-story, and heritage. Myers describes the importance of the therapist operating from an optimal worldview. That perspective creates an oppor-

24. Myers et al., "Recommendations Psychological Treatment," 14–15.
25. Akbar, *Psychological Slavery*.
26. Belgrane et al., *African American*, 29.
27. Myers, *Understanding Afrocentric*, 16.

tunity for persons to not only think critically but allows the therapist to engage African Americans in a way that affirms them and recognizes their diversity. Talmadge Anderson and James Steward highlight Wade Nobles understanding of the significance of black psychology.

Nobles states:

> Black psychology must concern itself with the question of "rhythm." It must discuss at some great length "oral tradition." It must unfold the mysteries of the spiritual energies now known as "the soul." It must explain the notion of "extended self" and the "natural" orientation of African people to ensure the "survival of the tribe." Briefly, it must examine the elements and dimensions of the experiential communalities of African people.[28]

Utilizing an African-centered approach not only begins with her-story, it will also speak to an African-centered worldview and spirituality that offer a holistic model of affirmation. This model promotes a healthy understanding of the identity of black women, re-educates and deconstructs negative identities internalized from others, and restores their identities, liberating and freeing them from harmful past identities, and journeying with them, all as this model affirms women's black and female identities.

Lastly, an African-centered approach acknowledges the relationship of black women and their faith. Akbar's framework for black psychology emphasizes the divine, and is reflective of nature and the natural order. His concept of the divine renders a deeper understanding of the self in connection to one's ancestors and the universe. Thus, he illustrates a concept of rhythm connecting persons of African descent, making visible the spirit of self that transcends the individual and seeks the communal. This free-flowing self is constant between self and nature. His interpretation is both conscious and unconscious, and is always active and seeking to thrive. Akbar reveals in his understanding of the psychology of black people that, in order to thrive in their natural state, they are most healthy when they are alive and connected to self, community, and God—because God is present in nature and community/relationships. This is important and viable when caring for black women in therapy as it invites their entire being—mind, body, soul, and experience—into the therapeutic space and creates opportunity for the therapist and counselee to form community and/or relatedness in the therapeutic encounter.

---

28. Anderson et al., *Introduction African American*, 177.

THEORETICAL AND THEOLOGICAL FRAMEWORK

Communal gatherings such as church and celebrations make space for this connection with self, others, and the divine to occur. An example of this can be seen in Morrison's *Beloved,* as Baby Suggs, (who today would be considered a preacher) gathers her congregation in the woods (nature). As they assemble in community, they are loving one another, self, and God.

Baby Suggs says:

> Let the children come.... Let your mothers hear you laugh.... Let the men come.... Let your wives see you dance.... Finally she called the women to her. Cry, she told them, for the living and the dead. And without covering their eyes the women cried.... It started that way: laughing children, dancing men, crying women and then it got mixed up. Women stopped crying and danced; men sat down and cried; children danced; women laughed; children cried.... In the silence that followed, Baby Suggs, holy, offered up to them her great big heart ... in this here place, we flesh; flesh that weeps, laughs; flesh that dances on bare feet in grass. Love it. Love it hard.[29]

The scene in *Beloved* in the woods with Baby Suggs not only demonstrates the relationship with the divine, it also shows how all people are connected with one another and thrive while singing, dancing, and crying in the presence of one another and God. Moreover, the scene makes evident how the grace of God was present and allowed each person to feel and experience the spirit of one another. When black women are able to express their faith belief in the therapeutic encounter, it allows for them to bring their entire being into the counseling moment. Thus, they can acknowledge and explore their faith and how they have used it as a means of coping. They can explore their faith and other means of coping in order to receive healing, wholeness, and transformation.

---

29. Morrison, *Beloved*, 103.

4

Research Methodology

MY RESEARCH METHOD IS a qualitative case study therapy group of six African American women who have experienced physical, emotional, and sexual forms of violence, and racism, classism, and sexism. The group met for two-hour sessions, twice a week for six weeks. An important approach to my clinical research with black women was to meet them where they were and begin with their narratives. This approach allowed them not only to give voice to the oppressive violence they have encountered, but also provided healing in the telling of their story.

Beginning with the black women's narrative demonstrates that the pastoral counselor is available to listen and, as a consequence, the counselee positions herself from invisible to visible. Listening and understanding are important to women who have been unheard, misrepresented, and invisible, invisible in relationship to others as well as to self. The theme of invisibility was shared during our third group session. Abbie, who is fifty-nine, explored how she isolated herself due to the racism she experienced in school, at home, and in her community. She wanted to be invisible so the name calling, finger pointing, and unsightly language used to describe her would stop. Creating a space for Abbie allowed her to value her feelings, engage her pain, and share her oppressive and negative experiences for the first time, thus authorizing her to become empowered through the telling of her-story. The case study method benefited Abbie, as well as the other group participants as it allowed for their human life experience to be heard. The clinical group, in conjunction with the journaling, allowed each group participant to be reflective and to raise questions within and after the group session ended.

RESEARCH METHODOLOGY

Clinical Group Case Study

The case study research method is defined as "an empirical inquiry that investigates a contemporary phenomenon (the "case") in depth and within its real world context, especially when boundaries between phenomenon and context may not be clearly evident"[1] This research method creates an opportunity for understanding the real and current lived experiences of black women from their perspectives. Additionally, the case study research method allows for the real life experience of black women to be heard, creates a space for each group participant to reflect on her story, and be supported/ provide support to others as they share their contextual story. The group therapy case study employed several phases:

- screening interviews
- group therapy meeting for two hours, twice a week for 6 weeks
- reflective journaling by participants
- clinical case study notes
- a research log by the researcher

A secondary approach to collecting data is the use of "ethnography as pastoral care." In her book *Ethnography as a Pastoral Practice: An Introduction,* Mary Clark Moschella *demonstrates how this type of story-hearing work can enable pastors and others in ministry to incorporate their listening skills to* gain insight into the people and communities they serve.[2] Moschella highlights that small gatherings not only create an intimate space for sharing, they also provide a space that is safe and inviting for others to share their story.[3] Additionally, that the role of listener requires us to give up the role of expert, and become a learner.[4]

The role of listener is important when working with black women because it validates their story. This is extremely important, not only because the researcher desires to learn of the women's experiences and create an empathic response that engages the participants to share their stories, but because the researcher also wants to learn from the women and create flexibility. This creates what Moschella describes as "suspending judgment and

1. Yin, *Case Study Research*, 16.
2. Moschella, *Ethnography*, 12.
3. Moschella, *Ethnography*, 13.
4. Moschella, *Ethnography*, 142.

going for fuller understanding."⁵ It allows women's narratives—the good, the bad, and the ugly—to unfold and be visualized by the hearers, thus allowing each participant to embrace and own their own story, and for the hearers to honor, witness, and accept the stories being told.

Allowing the eye witness—in this case, the researcher—to hear the testimony of the life experiences and the struggles of the group participants makes possible healing for the narrator and for the listeners. Moschella writes, "Our job is to notice as much nuance as possible, and to help a person magnify his [her] story, make it larger, clearer, and more available to the teller. The plot thickens, the mystery unfolds, and we witness a story in progress. We hear what is beautiful, agreeable, and pleasing. We listen also for "the contradictory, the unpleasant, the negative. We try not to censor the difficult details of the story, but to accept them without fear."⁶

Ethical Considerations

To ensure ethical responsibility, all of the participants were treated justly in accordance with the ethical guidelines set forth by Columbia Theological Seminary. To minimize risk, I worked with participants who were over the age of forty. The project was supervised by a faculty member of the department of pastoral care at the Interdenominational Theological Center (ITC), a licensed professional counselor, and a certified pastoral counselor.

The Role of the Researcher

I am an African American woman, ordained clergyperson, and doctor of theology candidate who seeks licensure as a marriage and family therapist. My role within the counseling process was to listen and interact as a participant observer and pastoral counselor.

Sample Selection and Consent Process

I began my research with an advertisement at the ITC, Atlanta, Georgia, to recruit participants. I followed up with screening interviews to determine suitability of prospective participants. The screening criteria included:

    5. Moschella, *Ethnography*, 143.
    6. Moschella, *Ethnography*, 143.

- African American female student at ITC who identifies herself as having some experience of violence and/or oppression
- No prior relationship to the researcher or the clinical consultant, Dr. CaTrice Glenn
- Further exploration of issues explored during the screening process are included in Sample Screening Questions in #10 below
- Emotionally stable enough to participate in a group (If in my judgment, the woman does not meet this criterion, I will make a therapy referral for her at the Thomas J. Pugh Center at ITC for free counseling.)

I conducted screening interviews on the campus for eight weeks during the fall semester of 2014, with the permission of the ITC president and faculty chair of the ITC pastoral care department. The therapy group began with eight participants and concluded with six active participants. The group met for two hours, twice a week for six weeks. The therapy group meetings took place at the Thomas J. Pugh Counseling Center on the ITC campus.

There are no known risks associated with the research prior to and after the conclusion of the group. Each participant was given the opportunity to give voice to their experience, and explore questions and experiences that may have been suppressed. Additionally, the project created opportunities for further research to help explore issues raised by the study as it relates to black women's experiences and communities. Moreover, the informed consent provided to each participant ensures that they are aware that their information will be protected by the researcher, and any audio recordings will be transcribed and then kept for five years in a locked and secure place according to the requirements of Columbia Theological Seminary. Data for analysis included (1) themes from the therapy sessions, (2) themes from a final evaluative wrap-up "good-bye" session with the participants to gain their evaluations of the therapy, and (3) contents of the researcher's research log.

Sample Screening Questions

1. Are you an African American woman student at ITC?
2. Have you ever experienced some form of violence and/or oppression?
3. Do you have any prior relationship to Rev. Malone or Rev. Glenn?

4. Have you experienced any form of racism, sexism, or classism?
5. Have you experienced sexual, physical, or emotional abuse?
6. Do you ever struggle with your identity as a black woman?
7. Do you consider yourself a strong black woman?
8. Do you ever believe there are other ethnicities more superior to you as an African American woman?
9. Do you know who you are as a black woman?
10. How much would you say you have been able to grieve or lament the negative experiences in your life?

Sample Questions and Issues Explored in Therapy Group

1. What generation (since the Emancipation Proclamation of enslaved Africans) are you in your family?
2. Were you raised by one or both of your parents?
3. Do you like yourself?
4. Have you ever been sexually abused or exploited?
5. Please define how you see or identify yourself.
6. Describe any negative images of yourself and where they came from.
7. When was the first time you were sexually exploited or taken advantage of?
8. Were you ever raped or molested?
9. Do you ever have low self-esteem?
10. (If yes to #4): How many abusive relationships have you been in?
11. Describe your feelings after your experience of racism, sexism or classism.
12. If you identify with the strong black woman image, do you feel you are always strong/always have to be strong?
13. How and when might you be able to grieve or lament?

Method of Data Analysis

The researcher's approach to data analysis was to observe each group participant's verbal and non-verbal communication. This allowed me as the participant observer and pastoral counselor to address unspoken and spoken themes demonstrated within the group. Information collected during this research was transcribed from themes from the therapy sessions, final evaluative wrap-up "good bye" session with the participants to gain their evaluations of the therapy; and contents of the researcher's research log. To interpret the data of the narratives, I investigated them utilizing a social and cultural lens. All data have been password protected and secured in a locked filing system. I used a qualitative method to explore the themes in the interpretation and data collection.

5

Research Findings

The Women's Experiences

"I feel fragmented; I don't know who I am. I was never asked."

—Diane

THE WOMEN OF AFRICAN descent that participated in this research project are all in ministry in various positions and callings within the black church. Each participant explored their experience of racism, sexism, and classism by white men and women, as well as black men and women. Four of the six women experienced sexual, emotional, and physical violence by white and black men and women. Each group participant explored her experience of institutional, religious, and societal racism, classism, and sexism. During the initial interview process, six of the eight original group participants had not received any form of counseling regarding their experiences of various forms of violence, racism, sexism, and classism. All participants shared that there was not adequate space in which they could openly share their experiences and feelings, and four of the eight shared that they have not experienced any safe space where they were able to lament and be vulnerable.

This section examines the voices of the women as they share their narratives and explore questions that speak to their experiences of violence and oppression. Additionally, this chapter introduces each group participant, and probes their initial interview, their reflective journaling, and the clinical group. The data process utilized for this section highlights the women's journey towards excavation of their internal and external feelings as it relates to their experiences of racism, sexism, classism, and violence. Additionally, it explores the role of God, Spirit, and/or church and the relationship of their faith in the journey towards healing. Each woman's name has been changed to ensure anonymity and security as they allow themselves to be vulnerable and transparent and express their feelings, thoughts, and concerns in the therapeutic space, as well as, through journaling. I introduce the six group participants—Abbie, Tanya, Karen, Olivia, Diane, and Erica—in the following section.

Initial Interview Process

During the initial screening interviews, the women participants disclosed the following: (1) they are students of ITC, (2) they have experienced some form of violence and oppression, (3) they do not have any prior relationships with this researcher or clinical supervisor Dr. Glenn, (4) they have experienced various forms of racism, sexism, and classism during their lifetime in the church and wider community, and (5) they have experienced forms of sexual, physical, spiritual, and emotional abuse. Each woman stated she did not struggle with her identity as a black woman, identifies herself as a strong black woman, does not believe that there are other ethnicities more superior to her as an African American woman, affirms who she is as a black woman, and some stated that they had ample spaces to lament the negative experiences in their life. Throughout this book these same statements were explored in more depth, and questions were raised by the group participants as they explored and gave voice to their experiences.

During the initial group session the women shared the following in response to several invitations and questions:

1. Please introduce yourself to the group.

Karen: Hi, I am Karen originally from Oakland, California. I have completed my graduate education here in Atlanta, received my first master's at Clark, my MDiv from ITC, and am working towards my DMin at ITC. Currently I am completing my CPE at Grady hospital in hopes of completing a residency in the fall. That is my current goal as I work towards licensure in the COGIC church to become a chaplain. I am forty-eight, never been married with no children, and live on campus.[1]

Tanya: Hello, my name is Tanya I am a second-year student at ITC from Jacksonville, Florida. I am AME, forty-one, divorced twice, and have

---

1. All quotations from this chapter were recorded during a series of interviews with the author from August 18 to November 10, 2014.

two children Chastity fifteen, Eddie twenty-two, and a granddaughter named Lisa who is the love and joy of my life. I am really excited to be here. My background is education and banking, and now I am pursuing a master of divinity and becoming more and more open minded to what will happen when I graduate.

Olivia: Greetings, I'm Olivia and I am a graduating senior, praise God. I'm sixty-three and I am a cross between Presbyterian and non-denomination because of the split between Johnson C. Smith and ITC, which has had a great impact on me right now because I am flip flopping both ways and plus my denomination is in Massachusetts and I am not a part of the Atlanta Presbytery. I am part of Southern New England Presbytery. I am divorced and have a twenty-nine-year-old son, David, who keeps me on track when I want to go off track.

Abbie: Hi everyone, I'm Abbie. This is my second year at ITC. I am sixty, divorced, and no children. I'm a licensed Apostolic minister, and this is my second career after being a nurse for thirty years and I moved here from California in 2008.

Erica: I'm Erica. I have two twin adult sons Stephen and James and a beautiful granddaughter Cynthia. I am originally from St. Louis, Missouri, been married twice—separated from second husband and a graduating senior at ITC. I am AME and have a 501(c) 3 business back home. This will be my second master's and I have a PhD. I'm fifty-five.

Diane: Hi. I'm Diane, AME pastor, wife of Donald and a DMin student here at ITC. I am forty-seven, no children and I moved here from Wisconsin. I was raised by military parents. I have two older brothers, and went to undergrad at Clark and I'm looking forward to the group.

2. Please define how you see or identify yourself.

Abbie: Well you know I have called myself an African American. I hadn't really defined that to myself. I was reading Lee Butler's *Liberating Our Dignity, Saving Our Souls* and he was sharing about how he looked at his African descendant and his American side and joined and married them together. I thought that was quiet interesting. I am still working on that. I use to identify myself as black, now I identify myself as African American, so it is still a working concept for me as how I would define myself in that arena, that's where I am in that. Wow. I think, it's been some time, God I would say it's been, I can't tell you how many years ago or anything like that it's when it became more prevalent is when I started to define myself as that. I remember when Dr. Matthews came to our classroom, she said you should always capitalize the b in Black, when there were many times I made it lower case which was very significant for me you know so when that came more popular is when I started using it because for a while there was a negative connotation. I can remember my cousin who was fair skin yellow tone, for lack of a better word might be the right way to say it, better word I thought she was better, than it appeared during that time that skin color in that day even today if you are light skin you are better. And so I always looked at myself as the dark one, everyone in my whole family was dark pretty much. It was a negative connotation with that so ever since it became popular to say Africa I have embraced that, define that for me I am still working on it.

Tanya: I was pretty excited when it was ok to identify yourself with Africa, more so from an elementary mental standpoint I was so tired of being called black big nose, black nerd, black white talking girl, black this black that, anything you could put after black. That's what I got, so then I was like as I have grown into an adult if you will, I know that I am not from Africa, have never been to Africa, but I am proud and more than willing to have the opportunity to marry that to what I know as far as for someone who has lived in America all her entire life. And I think that part of it since I've never been there is so much I do not know I cannot identify from a cultural stand point. But it's really an honor to have a legacy to even attach myself to as taught here in America about who we are and who came before us and it was all just real bad and it was bad for a long time. Definitely respecting them for the struggle but felt like there has to be something better. There has to be more and this has been recently, even going to Florida University for an undergrad 94/96 the skin color deal was major at that even being at an HBCU it was still a struggle. And there wasn't the pride at high school it was even worse and going forward I went to a white college to earn my first master's and then ITC. I am grateful for every knock upside the head I am also grateful for the opportunity to still choose what to do for my life and my hair and still have the freedom to do that.

Karen: For me it was different in elementary school. We had teachers who were from the regime of black pride just on the end of Black Panther movement. In south central LA they had a home office. We received food from that movement as far as feeding kids in school so the teachers from that movement taught us who we were. They showed us books from Africa, they had maps of Africa, and they made you proud of being who you are. When I got older they taught that you are African, black is a color, in the crayon show flesh tone like peach color so why is flesh tone if I'm not my color? So how is that flesh tone you show the difference America is showing you who's prominent who's not who's worthy and who's not, so you have knocked out the majority of the population in our community they changing the color and now it's peach so I embraced that the older I got. Living in south LA you had to find your niche. There is not a black community. In south LA there is not a black community, a two block radius, we don't have our own town, so it was important to me to find a place that looked like me so I got my bachelor's, I wanted to get my master's but I wanted to get it at an all-black university. I had never had that experience. I went to all-girls school got my BA, I had gone to Fresno and took a couple courses, it wasn't working for me you know because what I needed was something that responds to me. So I enrolled in Clark. That was an awesome experience for me. It was in Atlanta that I saw black family and folk doing something positive and it reminded me of Compton when I was a little girl. When I visited Big Mama and saw her cooking Christmas dinner every holiday—you know you had a meal, I guess I've been back and forth so I think Atlanta is home now. I love the vibe; you can be African American here and be ok. Your name is so important to you—whatever you let somebody call you that's what you value, so be careful what you let somebody call you. Make sure people respect your name. I got that being here in Atlanta and then at ITC being knocked in the head—you were reminded of who you are and your cultural heritage. They taught me here at Clark and ITC to be proud of who I am. So going back to the first question, I identify as African American, because my roots are Africa and I was reared and raised here although I may not ever get to Africa I honor that, I am African American.

Olivia: Well you know growing up in Alabama, in the middle of segregation you had colored when my dad raised us in a sheltered life. Because of fear he kept saying he lived a hard life. I didn't understand that cause we didn't talk about color. We were Christians. We went to church on Sundays. It was church and home or school and home, so it wasn't a thing that we sat and talked about. My dad said he was raised up with white families and they played together. I left at age eighteen. My dad told me to stand for what you believe in and that has traveled with me all these years. He taught us about community and love. We knew of the hard life he told us about but not racism. It wasn't until I left home that I experienced that I was black and that racism existed. When I left home at eighteen I was slapped in the face by a white girl who called me black. I thought to myself I am not black, I didn't know what color was. My momma was Indian and my dad was black but we never discussed it. So this changing who I am has been a struggle and is still a struggle so if I had to identify myself I would say that I'm a Christian. I was questioned about my culture and who I am here at ITC. It has made me look at why I am so negative about color. I had to write a paper once. I said I don't know who I am and one instructor told me I was a black female. I had to analyze it. Okay, a black female. I looked at my birth certificate and it said colored. I had to challenge her and say show me where it tells me I'm black. I would love to go to Africa to see where I came from, but I don't grab on to what you tell me. This is who I am, a child of God, I don't know as far as color.

Erica: African American female, African descendant. For many years I have defined myself as African-America female. Prior to that I have a very Afro-centric father, Garvey-like, and my mother's family was Creole. They talked about race, but not as much as my father talked about race in our household. He was always discussing race and race issues. My parents met in Mississippi and my father moved closer to my mother's home during the time of segregation. They were both teachers. My dad was born in Ohio and he had different perspective so he got involved in things that my mom didn't. I was born in Mississippi and raised in St Louis. My siblings were raised in Mississippi and they have a different experience than I do. In our home my father taught black history so I grew up and we had black pictures, my sisters had black waking dolls that I used to cut the hair and eyelashes off. My father interestingly, talked about race all the time. The way I was raised put me in a strange situation. I grew up with a father who says things like "the average black man," "the average white man," and he would make concrete statements about black and white, and I grew up believing it to be true.

3. Do you ever struggle with your identity as a Black woman?

Tanya: For me I would say yes. It has not been easy growing up with a darker complexion. I have been called every name in the book and they just put black in front of it and said it. As I am older, I am embracing more of being identified as African American but the struggle with beauty is still there. I was criticized by blacks for not being black enough and the boys didn't want to date me cause I was dark. However, I was the one they wanted to screw on the side cause they thought I was exotic. They would say things like, "You kind of sexy to be dark skinned." They talked about my nose, my lips, the color of my skin, and my hair. You name it they talked about it. All of what people say—I began to question was I a freak.

Researcher: Can you tell us how you define freak?

Tanya: I guess a freak is the opposite of the norm or what is considered beautiful—I questioned my mom who called me beautiful. I would say to myself so wait a minute if I'm beautiful—where am I getting my definition from—so if we were reading beauty, then whoever is reading it their face should pop up. It's as if we are given beauty categories and everybody can't fit into that definition of beauty given by society. Today people look at me and say, "You don't have issues with men," "You don't have issues with beauty," "You don't have problems with self-esteem," and I'm just like please, inside.

Karen: We have been under the oppression of society to embrace what culture says. You have to embrace what beauty looks like which is long blonde hair and blue eyes. Or in our own community, beauty was three shades lighter than a paper bag. It wasn't easy growing up as a black female because you were judged by how you looked. I was the underdog and didn't fit with the status quo and the culture. I know that we have to be freed as people of color, not assimilate, and become stronger. When we do this we will become stronger and be able to deal with our woundedness and hurt.

Researcher: How did it make you feel growing up as a black girl?

Karen: Sad. It's sad cause we have to get years of therapy cause it has impacted us so much. You know I have a sister who is bright skin and so growing up I wasn't fussed over, I was told that I had to be smart because I was dark skinned and I wasn't pretty. I would have to take care of myself. I love my sister who is light skinned with fine hair. However, it's taken me years to get to a place that I was able to love and accept myself.

Olivia: My sisters called my son names cause he was black. They would say things like, "I can't see you, why don't you smile?" I think that is why I identify as an American cause they have been so evil and what I experienced growing up in the South—they were so mean.

Researcher: How does that make you feel?

Olivia: It made me angry. I never wanted my son to suffer. I wanted him to fit in and have the best, like everyone else. That is why I scrubbed floors, sewed clothes, sold dinners, so he could have anything he dreamed.

And today when I see dark skinned young men my heart goes out cause I know what my son went through and how hard it was growing up and how hard it was being black and so I admire them and now I am encouraging young black girls.

Researcher: And what about you? You shared about your son. I would love to hear about you.

Olivia: Well, I guess I never others and judged by my skin color. It makes me sad that people don't get to know questioned who I was or looked at color cause my dad said we were Christians and that is how I identified until I left home and learned that I was different than you. They just judge you, especially other black women.

Researcher: Tell me more about being judged by other black women.

Olivia: Well, I never really fit in—in my family or the church. My sisters didn't like me cause they said I was different. I always gave and did but they have always judged me cause I was different. No support. I kinda dressed how I wanted to dress and did things my way and they always criticized me for that. And being a pastor's wife I didn't dress the way they thought I should dress and they judged me for that, too. I have always did what I wanted cause my dad said that I could be anything. But I was judged for not being like other women. You know how they dressed or looked, stuff like that. You know cause I sew and quilt and make clothes. I was outside of the box. I wore what I like and didn't try to fit in and they said I was different. I'm learning that I have to accept I'm different and that's fine with me.

Researcher: How does being different make you feel?

Olivia: I feel sorry for them that they can't accept women that's different from them.

Researcher: I want to confirm your difference and ability to be outside of the box. I also wanted to know, do you accept yourself? You don't have to answer now but I want to encourage you to reflect and journal what comes up for you.

Olivia: I'll reflect more, but I think I accept myself, but I do struggle.

Karen: Sometime we can be our worst enemy. But I think its cause we were put against one another during slavery, which continues today. We have the light skin versus the dark skin, long hair versus short hair, and good hair versus bad hair. Slavery really messed us up, but we ain't talking about it. As women we need to come together, but first we have to deal with our pain. You know the saying, *hurt people hurt people.*

Diane: I had a different experience from the other women. Everywhere my parents were stationed. I wasn't exposed to all of that. However, I did have a culture shock when they were stationed in Wisconsin. I was the only black person. I felt I had to compete cause I wanted friends and I wanted them to like me. I believe that the negative stuff from the media about black people shaped how they saw all black people. I remember when we moved to Atlanta, I asked my mom where all these black people come from. I had never seen or been around so many black people. I can relate to Tanya cause growing up I remember hearing, "The darker the berry the sweeter the juice," and someone else would say, "But if it gets too dark it ain't no use." But I negated all that because I believe that dark-skinned is beautiful. Assumptions shouldn't be made cause I know dark and light skin have been mistreated and been called bad names. But it wasn't my skin color that caused me not to fit in so much but my multiple sclerosis.

Researcher: What was that like for you?

Diane: It was painful. I was twenty-three and my world changed. I had to struggle with a new identity cause of this diagnosis which I am able to refer to now as dis-ease. But it took a while to get here. I mean I was so angry I didn't know why this happened to me. What I have come to know is that giving up is not an option.

Researcher: What does giving up look like for you?

Diane: Letting my diagnosis rule me. People used to say I'm praying that God heals you but it all depends how you look at healing. There is a physical healing and a spiritual healing. And I'm healed spiritually. Although I have my days, I'm able to deal with the pain and not allow it to control my life. I can still do things just like anyone else. I may not do it as fast but I can do it and I have learned that I just have to go at my own pace.

Researcher: Sounds like you have learned how to accept and embrace your dis-ease?

Diane: I have. It's a part of who I am and I'm at peace with it.

Erica: Well growing up I was taught that black was beautiful. It was only outside of the home that I struggled cause it was the opposite. It hasn't been easy being a black woman, especially for darker skinned black women, and I believe that as a result of racism and other isms, black women had to be stronger in order to survive and it is perceived that darker women had to work harder than light-skinned women.

Karen: Well, I have a sister who looks patty white and she would fit in the social clubs here in the South. You know that Jack and Jill social club. The legacy at Spelman and Morehouse. You know they are only a few generations from slavery cause they so light with the fine hair. You have to be invited into it—you know it's based on money and color. You know it's about how you look—sororities also play a role but it's just the south.

Researcher: Tell me what feelings are coming up for you?

Karen: It makes me want to scream that we do this to each other. Like in Ferguson but we are not talking about the six people who were killed by our own. We need to deal with the internal issues—we need to deal with our own isms. I'm frustrated thinking about the good old boy positions. It's frustrating that people who are darker had to work harder—that's why affirmative action was so important until somebody stepped up and said we don't need that.

Researcher: How has your life been as a darker woman? How have you been affected by what you have shared?

Karen: It made me fight harder for me to know who I was as a darker skinned sister. It caused me to realize and deal with the fact the oppression is very real by others and by blacks towards other blacks.

Researcher: During the session there has been some references made to colorism and hair. Can you share what it feels like sitting in this space with the therapist who can be described as light skinned or two shades lighter than a paper bag with long, fine hair?

Olivia: I have a question. What is your nationality?

Researcher: I am African American.

Olivia: I asked cause when I first met you when you interviewed me you reminded me of my best friend who was from Cape Verde. Also I connected with you cause you were from New Jersey.

Tanya: My mom has a lot of pain that she never dealt with. She is darker than I am but she doesn't receive that she is beautiful. I heard stories of how those "yellow girls Nana did this to me and that to me." She was mistreated by white women and black women who had lighter skin with fine hair. I had it bad, but not as bad as my mother cause I had good grades—kinda what Karen talked about I wasn't pretty so I wanted to be smart. There was an assumption that light-skinned girls thought they were better than dark-skinned girls until I met my best friend who is light-skinned with fine hair. Her name is Lisa. I remember when I became principal or when I was a high school teacher, I had to reframe how I saw white people. I used to refer to them as pilgrims and I had to learn how to be nice/nasty with them and their responses towards me. But the real change came when my son would bring his friends home who were all pilgrims. I mean what did I expect him to do? We lived in a white neighborhood and I sent him to all-white schools cause I wanted to protect him and keep him away from violence. So I had to re-think what I felt about pilgrims and work on not referring to calling white people pilgrims, cause I loved all my babies and my son's friend Stephen would call himself my vanilla son.

So dealing with my students and my son's friends helped me to change my thinking. When I first saw you I thought was my granddaughter Allison going to have fine hair like yours. Her mom is white—I mean how can I raise my granddaughter so she is grounded and embraces both ethnicities, her black and white side. Now a couple of years ago I would have been like how she gonna wanna talk about oppression she don't know nothing about oppression. Oh God, how this yellow girl gonna talk to us about our experiences she can't relate. But the Lord has a strange sense of humor teaching us that everything we thought we knew could be turned upside down. Being open allows for you to get a new perspective. Because I would shudder to think that my grandbaby would have to deal with people like how I was.

Diane: When I came in I was ready to give you a hug. You have been a pleasure from our interviews and when you checked on me when I got sick before group started. I did think that you were gonna look different cause of the topic we were discussing—kinda like a darker-skinned sistah. And when we first met, I did say to myself I wonder if she is even black, or mixed with black and white cause your hair texture. I remember hearing the saying like, "Bright light damn near white." But I just thought, wow, she got us all here and everybody is darker than her.

Abbie: I thought you were beautiful and that you had pretty hair. Wasn't really sure if you were African American. I didn't really think anything bad or negative. Looking forward to what you have to say about oppression.

Karen: I first felt connected knowing you were from ITC. I guess for me knowing that you graduated from ITC, I thought, wow, she graduated and has come back to address some issues so I thought that was awesome. Cause we know we have issues in our community because of slavery and we haven't dealt with them yet. Our men and our relationships to our men, self, and community. We have basically been told get over it. So what you've been raped. You've been abused. Get over it. So to come back at a time when we are going through a crisis at ITC and in the black community says that you care about rebuilding and that is a necessary conversation to have at this present moment and that's why I am here. Now if you had not graduated from ITC and was coming from Columbia I would have been like, who she think she is coming to get information from us about oppression. But now I think what you are doing is great and needed cause we don't have spaces where we can talk about us or our experiences as black women.

Erica: I learned a long time ago that perceptions can be misleading so I didn't think too much about it. What led me here is the topic and the need to discuss issues that have been buried for so long. Healing needs to take place within us and in our community and that is why I am here. But when I first met you I said that you had a beautiful spirit and I'm glad that you are willing to explore this topic as it has been skated over and swept under the rug. It's needed at this place in history right now dealing with everything that being thrown in our face we can't deny it any longer.

Researcher: Thank you all for your openness and transparency and trusting me enough to share your feelings and concerns.

4. Have you ever experienced any form of racism, sexism, or classism?

Erica: Yes, growing up I wasn't able to have the same experience as my sisters. They were able to go to a segregated school and be taught by black teachers who cared—and I didn't and I feel like the teachers treated the black kids differently and that they didn't care. Growing up in a home that discussed race, I never really thought about if I was dark skinned until I moved to St. Louis and was a part of segregation. The whites were adamant about blacks going to their own neighborhood schools. My siblings were much older and didn't have to experience the segregation in the school system. The neighborhoods were changing when blacks moved in whites moved out. The neighborhoods were changing overnight. I remember having to be bused to a white school so it could be integrated and it was so bad they would throw rocks at our bus—just like you see in the movies. I got hit in the lip with a rock and my parents took me out of that public school and put me in a Lutheran school in the same neighborhood. I was the only black in the class. I continued to experience racism. It was just subtle and weird. They would put my class picture in the center, it was things that you would notice and zero in on. I was in there from fourth to eighth grade then other blacks started to come and it became 20 to 30 percent black.

I couldn't wait to go to a black school. I couldn't wait to leave the Lutheran high school. It was so racist and we were made to feel like aliens. In the seventies, there were scholarships given to black kids to attend white schools, but I went to black college and wanted to intentionally work for a black company as a result of my childhood experience. It was just normal everything going on around me in my home was positive about our race all my life and when I got to school it was the opposite. I was engaged in race, St. Louis was a horrible place to be engaged in race. A lot of separatism on purpose, very intentional. Everything was race. A lot of the things I did growing up I was always placed with white people. When I became a teacher of African American studies is when I was able to learn balance, although I knew black is beautiful—I had to learn balance. Because I was like my dad over the edge, he taught that just because you love yourself doesn't mean you have to hate others. I had to learn to balance. Some of that came from my mother because of her father, because he wanted to own land. He kept getting burned out. He would move and buy land. They would steal his cows. My father was a football coach. He was fired. The school superintendent was the wife of the bank president. They would tell him what not to do and he didn't, so he got fired.

Olivia: I got slapped in the face with racism when this white girl called me a nigger when I was eighteen. I was ready to fight, but my sister pulled me back—yeah that's a fighting word. Growing up in Alabama in the 50s and 60s in segregation it was distinguished between whites and blacks. My father raised us in a sheltered life cause of fear. He kept saying, "I lived a hard life," but I didn't understand what that meant when he use to talk to us until I left home and experienced racism for myself when I moved to Massachusetts, which is one of the racist states. It was different in Alabama because we lived in our own neighborhood and was segregated. We went to school and church and home. I guess when I moved I wasn't expecting it. But I have experienced racism by my other black women, too. I feel like it was cause I was different. I don't know what it was cause they just didn't like me.

Tanya: Yes, I think my mom's image of herself cause of racism and my experiences have impacted me. My mom tried to help me when I was teased and picked on about how I looked but because she never really dealt with her own experience I don't know if that's why I didn't believe that I was beautiful. Our black men choosing white or light women. It's been a lot of pain over the short span of my life. Even though people say I talked like a white girl I don't know if that is why maybe I was rejected by black boys. Well, they wanted sex cause of my color but—being of a darker tone you are faced with oppression more maybe. I live in neighborhoods with pilgrims and worked with pilgrims but it was my people that just didn't accept me. Even though pilgrims had issues with me I learned how to be nice nasty to deal put my own and black men it's just too much.

Karen: Society, but I have learned how to exist. Most recently though my church cause they don't ordain women. COGIC is very oppressive here in Atlanta. Now I'm struggling to leave and go back to the Baptist church to be licensed cause it's so oppressive only if I allow it to be oppressive. It's enough work in the church for women they don't need to be licensed—then they would be equal to me this is a statement made by mother Sally who is over the women's ministry. They are not forcing the men to respect them as full citizens they are okay with being eye candy on their man's arm. I believe you are not fully walking in your destiny if you are not being treated equally. I made a decision to walk away cause I don't think the gift God gave me should be extinguished cause the church won't ordain me. I didn't allow that to hinder my relationship with God—so I'm working around man-made rules cause God poured his spirit on men and women.

Erica: I find the church to be oppressive in general. My husband is an Apostolic elder and he uses the word woman like it's a pejorative. He is deeply rooted in traditionalism. He was raised COGIC and now Apostolic. It kills my spirit when he would say I'm wrong for having an opinion. He is a male dominance and chauvinistic. That relationship causes me to struggle with "what is Gods will for women." I felt suffocated—I had to be submissive. He would say things like God don't speak to you he speaks to the husband. But he thought he was respecting me that is the funny thing. He didn't think there was anything wrong with it cause that is how he was taught. It's like somebody was putting a pillow over my head.

Abbie: My license had to be renewed but I didn't see that as being oppressive until all the ministers who had to have their license renewed was sitting in the front of the church and he didn't call everybody up and I was one of them. Another incident was when I was wearing a short sleeve dress. It was respectful. Nothing was showing but my arms and you would have thought I didn't have any clothes on. It wasn't until I left and experienced something different that I realized that it was oppressive—but when I was there I didn't. Now that I'm gone I feel free.

Tanya: I thought it was interesting that I could not recall an experience of oppression. I have been reflecting on that to see if I'm just pushing it down—but it is something that I'm thinking about.

Olivia: I have experienced racism here in Atlanta. I have constantly been told I'm different and I need to discover my culture. I guess I'm not black enough for them, but it's not my color, it's me, cause I'm different and have my own style and don't dress like them.

Diane: As an African American woman, I have been discriminated against in the church—twenty years at one church, ordained for twelve years, but no leverage because of my disability. I don't call it a disease I call it a dis-ease cause I'm not at ease when something happens—there is nothing I can't do I might can't do it at the rate you do it, but give me a minute if it's something I wanna do I'll do it. I feel angry but I didn't let it show I was never utilized to do anything in the church.

Tanya: I think more than anything we give so much life to words and words are powerful and we can choose what we give life to—words that come from others or come from ourselves. I had a friend here at ITC text me and say that they were praying for me because I was being under attack so I texted them back and said, "under attack???" I didn't know that I was under attack. I knew that I was dealing with issues, but it's very seldom that I will label anything an attack. It was tragic when my daddy died—but he was old and I got to spend time with him and he knew I loved him. Even though our ancestors were oppressed they took a different spin on it and turned it around and said but God loves me, so that was affirming to them. They didn't value what those who had oppressed them and said about God. They knew God for themselves and that was affirming because God loved them. My mom would say, "Sticks and stones may break your bones but words will never hurt me." But when the name-calling came it was ugly and I mean ugly and it hurt me to the core. As an adult I was like that is foolishness to me because the words did hurt but she would say that I'm beautiful. Now on Facebook some of the same people who were so mean to me would try and talk to me after taunting me for years. I was the one that they guys wanted to screw on the side cause they saw me and thought that I was exotic because of my skin color—dark—and now they send me messages you kinda sexy to be dark—but they use to talk about my nose, lips, the color of my skin, and my hair. These features haven't changed. I'm still the same with the same looks and darker skin. All of what people say would cause you to say well who the freak am I—who are you. So I wait a minute and say well am I beautiful. Where am I getting my definition of beauty from? So if we were to read beauty, then whoever is reading it, then their face should pop up. It's as if we were given beauty categories and everybody can't fit into that definition of beauty. You don't have issues with men and beauty. People would say to me you don't have a problem with getting a man, you don't have low self-esteem, and that I don't have problems or issues with beauty. But they just don't know.

Karen: I would contend that your beauty hasn't changed, but the people looking at you now have been freed from the oppression of society. We have to get to a place where we don't embrace what culture has to say about what beauty is and that is the challenge. Cause we all can't be a size four with blonde hair and blue eyes. That ridiculous. My boyfriend now, we couldn't be together in school cause he was the big buff football player and had it going on and I was the smart girl who didn't or wasn't in clicks. We were different people back then but now we are able to be together cause we don't have to put on a façade. We all can't be three shades lighter than a paper bag with long hair. And yes, their image of beauty affected my self-esteem. Back then my self-esteem was low because I was defined by society and culture. I didn't have the fashion and didn't look the part. We don't lean towards the underdog cause we wanna be embraced by the status quo and culture. We have to find ourselves. We have to be strong and get to a place and know who we are and get through that stuff cause we've all been wounded and hurt. And so we walking around wounded and hurt.

5. Describe your feelings after your experience of racism, sexism, or classism?

Tanya: For me it would have to be the stereotype of the angry black woman. I think the whole label is like any stereotype that has been used to define us as we have been oppressed and subsequently became angry. It does not represent all of who we are. However, I do believe that we are certainly more passionate. I believe we have more depth based on our past and our ancestry that makes us a more complex woman. There are a lot of black women who are extremely voiceless about their opinion to the point where it's like a film placed over the entire race.

Abbie: I held my anger a lot cause I was married to a monster and I didn't want the church people to see the angry black woman. But my husband did a lot of dirt, a lot of dirty stuff whereby he devalued me at church, he devalued me in public, and in front of his friends. So, um, when I divorced him I left Massachusetts and went to Decatur, Alabama, and told him I wanted him to sell the house. But he flip-flopped on me and as soon as I left he brought his girlfriend in to my house to live. The house went into foreclosure and he filed bankruptcy and named me as one of his creditors after I put him through school to get his PhD, and I got stuck with a $35,000 loan. So it put a damper on things for me financially and then I lost the house I purchased in Alabama. Since then he has been married five times and has not helped me with our son. After all that, I used laughter to deal with my anger. It is how I coped with my anger and I'm working on giving myself the okay to express my anger.

Karen: To a degree I identify with the angry black woman. I think that most stereotypes are some little kernel of truth and it got used to exploit for other people's purpose. I think historically, black women have been angered and have been treated in ways where they would become angry. And if they didn't get angry at ways in which we have been treated it would be a concern for me because anger would be the appropriate response. I know that because I am one of them. Um, the righteous indignation. We are one of the people who have been exploited and used for the purpose and pleasure of other people. We have been sought after for abuse, control, and damaged for the purpose of others. The control and the ways in which we have been damaged and I used to be what I like to call a "bodacious" angry black woman because we've had to be that. Sometimes I want to say listen up. We were not born angry, but all that has happened to us shapes and informs us and when we look historically we see black women who have been stereotyped as angry black women because they were more vocal.

Abbie: It takes me a while to get angry. Because when I get angry its cause the pain is too great to bare. Sometimes the pain looks like loneliness and causes me to go to God more and it causes me to start searching within myself and look at those things I have become uncomfortable with, like the other day when my pastor said something to me it caused me to reflect on where I'm at and my feelings. As so, of course for me it builds up and so when I took the opportunity to look at it was kind of freeing. Admitting the feelings of rejection, un-forgiveness, low self-esteem, root of bitterness—and the list goes on—are things that I have mostly identified with me. And doing this is helping me to feel freer. Really looking inside myself and then I had to share that with God because there were some things I just didn't address—whatever caused the pain or if it caused me to feel uncomfortable and I would pull back and I wouldn't address it and I would close my eyes to it more so I'm learning how to sit and feel uncomfortable. To look at that is freeing cause I'm able to deal with when I'm rejected. And dealing with how rejection makes me fail like a failure because I made a mistake or if a person made a negative comment to me and I would think they were right. And so it's been a struggle, but reflecting and journaling has helped to look at that. So dealing with my experiences of oppression and dealing with my anger from it is freeing.

6. How and when might you be able to grieve or lament?

Tanya: For me what I got a revelation reading Psalm 77. The speaker starts out lamenting. He is having a very difficult time and as I continue to read through the psalm I can see where at a certain verse it is clear things had been well before, and now he is at the point where he is questioning God. He asks a series of questions to God regarding God's faithfulness, God's love and, um, God spurning and God being forever angry with him—you know cause he is basically looking at his situation not being well anymore as God is showing some type of vengeful wrath against him. So he is questioning who God is at this moment. As the psalm goes on he then starts to recall and remember what God has done. The things he has witnessed and he goes back to the exodus and when the children of God was led out of Egypt and even in that, God was with them. And that was a promise that was made to them and even now they can recall that promise. So for me I'm grateful for the opportunity to be given this space to talk through the thoughts in my head and my feelings.

Abbie: For me there are times when I screamed and hollered at God. And one time I heard, "I can hear you." So for me I think it's my getting to know God. I don't know if I'm placing a value judgment on God or doubting or is it me getting to God becoming who God wants me to be what I need at that time. I know that God will allow me to have these tantrums. It helps me to know that he is there and God allows me to talk it out until I get an understanding of what God is saying to me. So I thank you for allowing us a space to talk it out. But when I'm able to have a moment, it's a private moment between me and God. I know sometimes I can be in this space and now I'm learning how to turn stuff over to him and say let your will be done. And in time (weeping) I'm starting to see his comfort, his grace, his compassion, and his mercy, whereas initially I didn't see that I cause I was in this thing too deep. I remember going through my divorce and I asked him how he could allow this to be in the Bible. But in that process I found out that it's okay to cry. It's okay to struggle. It's okay to walk by faith, but to see in that moment what God is doing and learning how to gather peace even though I don't like the situation. I have been able to say, "God I don't like it." I have learned how to humble myself in that so God could minister to me in my lamenting.

Tanya: I don't know if I shared this but when I came here I was able to come because my daughter left. She wanted to live with her father in Atlanta. Before that, my son left prematurely and then my daddy died, all in a two-year period. The three people who I was closest to dipped on me [eyes tearing]. It was the worst time in my life. I never felt so alone, so lost, so confused and insignificant, so un-needed, so unloved. I had never ever felt that way. It was the lowest point in my life and it felt like it happened all in a matter of minutes. So now I'm here and I questioned God about the manner that I got here. God, I knew that it would be necessary in order for me to be here. When I got here it was such a disarray, it was like, I know I'm supposed to be here but this is some bull crap and I knew why I was here. I know there is calling on my life and the opportunity for me at thirty-nine to have the opportunity to go full time without any responsibility, and how does that happen.

It wasn't planned. My daughter left in June and I quit my job and left in July. My daughter's dad got her to believe that I put her off so I could move here—but it wasn't the truth. I had planned on going online. I had even moved away from the pilgrims to be closer to my mom and in my own community, so I could have support. And they told me at that last minute, and they didn't even give me time to process that my baby was leaving me. I had to go through her hating me—she used to look at me with disdain. I wanted to put my foot down. You gonna stay. But my pastor told me it was something I would have to pray about. From that Thursday to that Sunday, it was like a whirlwind. All I could do was cry. I felt like I didn't have a choice and I resented God for that.

Researcher: Did you tell God?

Tanya: Yes, I did. I don't even understand why you did it like that and that Sunday when her up. I was so angry I didn't know if I was going to make it. My mom said that she was going to baker act me (an act of involuntary surrender), but God and that was 2013.

Researcher: When you lamented, was it public and was it for a day or a period of time?

Tanya: It's private. It comes in spurts. I'm still lamenting, I mean I was just wailing and I just cry when I feel heavy and my mom would say, "I don't blame you. I know it must be painful and it was just all too much." It's all of that, daddy being gone, Chastity being gone, and Eddie leaving. It's like a period of grief. It comes and goes. I used to be like, I should be better by now, and then I took a class with Dr. Matthew and she said, "Who told you?" teaching us that there is no limit and that it was okay. So when I have moments of "you should be better by now," I know I'm in my pain and I'm not so hard on myself. But sometimes I would be depressed and now it's like when they come I know exactly why and I would tell myself to cry, go ahead and get it out. And then I pray cause I have to move forward cause it's never a functioning medium. So when I'm at that low, I have to put a valve on me and find something to have some joy about—and recall that God is in this. And I think about my daughter cause she is doing well. She has her issues about how she looks at me, but she is doing good in school. She will be 16 in August and seems to be adjusting.

Researcher: How do you deal with how she looks at you?

Tanya: I'm dealing cause I know that there is nothing I could do. I'm praying that what I have instilled in her won't be too far back in her mind. I realize that I can't control how she feels. I just continue to call and text and let her know that I love her and wait for her to call. Before I was able to take her phone, but I can't cause she not here with me.

Olivia: Well I've never been given the opportunity to grieve or lament. I mean I had to work and focus on taking care of my son. And when I shared my feeling with others I have always had to justify my feelings, my value, and worth to others. And that makes me angry.

Researcher: And what do you do when you become angry?

Olivia: When I become angry, I turn to my Bible and start reading. It helps me deal with being angry, cause I don't ever want the anger to take me to a place. I feel God is the only one who can help me when I am angry.

Erica: I feel like I have spaces to lament. But I tend to wear myself down until my body shuts down, and then I may talk to someone. But by then I am sick, when I keep going and have not gotten the rest I need or deal with why I am constantly giving.

Researcher: What do you feel when giving to others?

Erica: I feel good. I feel like I can say yes until it hurts. I guess I need to think about that more. I have learned that giving to others makes them feel good and that makes me feel good. I don't know. I'm a giver. That is how I was raised. Being the youngest, I did for others. I guess I carry it over and I have to work on finding balance and learn how to say no, and that it's okay.

Tanya: In this space I feel safe, but at the same time, I'm not so sure that I want to share. What I'm thinking is you coming down my street, so to speak, where I am able to cry out. And so I guess I'm trying to prepare myself for that. In our last session, the heaviness was there for me to share, but I didn't know what to do with that. I guess I'm feeling skeptical cause I'm not sure where my experience is going to take me, cause a lot of what I have shared thus far I have never shared before.

Researcher: And how does that make you feel?

Tanya: It makes me scared. Scared of being naked or vulnerable.

Researcher: And what do those feelings represent for you?

Tanya: Weakness. I don't know what to do with that because I don't have time to be weak. I just can't be weak.

Researcher: And what would happen if you allowed yourself to be weak?

Tanya: I may fall out crying and not be able to get back up. And what good would that do me?

Researcher: I want to encourage you to explore that further, and also reflect on where you received your interpretation of what is weak. And I'm here if you need me after you reflect more.

Tanya: Thanks. I'll do that—you know no one has asked me that before. I feel as if you are giving me permission to feel.

Researcher: Do you need permission?

Tanya: I guess I do?

Researcher: I encourage you to acknowledge your feelings to yourself, and that it's okay to feel whatever you feel.

Karen: I use worship to lament. That's the time I am able to express myself to God and deal with things that I am holding to. But I also have friends that I can talk to and be myself with. It's hard being in ministry cause when people see you they think that you don't go through. But yes, I'm able to lament and have done so in public and private.

Diane: I know, cause it's challenging trying to pastor two churches and be a wife. And when I have my moment's cause of the MS I need to be able to express myself. Well, I have my husband. He is very supportive. But a group like this would be helpful for clergy, cause we don't have this. I want to be able to curse or share how I feel without being judged. I feel like I'm wearing masks.

Tanya: I was in a worship experience on Ash Wednesday and it was said that we walk around here like we don't have a care in the world. We put on our faces—smiles and knowing that we are hurting in the inside. We put on makeup and dress up to make us look good and I said, "Well what are we supposed to do? Are we supposed to look like we are going through?" I have decided how I'm going to go through. There are many things that I thought long and hard about—the things in my life now could cause me to walk around crying with my head down. But there is a choice I made of how I'm going to go through. I could think negative about what causing me to go through, but I'm not cause that is not going to change anything.

Yesterday was a really tough day for me. I cried so much I thought I was dehydrated. And I thanked God before I went to bed. Thanking him for brand new mercies and allowing me to make it through the day. And then I went to bed. I woke up lighter. The problems was still there, but I put on my eyeliner and put on something half-way decent. And I don't think that that's putting on a façade. It's not like I lied and said I was okay. There are issues, but I am well. It's about how we go through. Does it enhance our walk or challenge our walk? I do my best to be pleasant as much as possible. But I'm told that that's fake.

Researcher: What feelings are coming up for you?

Tanya: I'm pissed. cause we always have something to say to one another. Why can't we just support one another? I don't think it's wrong. And we are just so judgmental in the church. Dianne, you should be able to curse, or whatever, to express yourself. And we do need a space for us.

Abbie: I remember when I was going through the divorce. For a while there, it was very difficult. And one day, I looked in the mirror and I said, "Oh my God, Abbie, you look bad. What happened to you?" And so I asked my pastor have I been looking this bad. cause for a while, I was really, really depressed. I didn't want to get out of the bed. I didn't want to face the world. I could barely bring myself to put clothes on. And even when I went to work, I would go into the linen closet cause I would start crying at any moment.

After a year of going through, and after visiting my family during Christmas that year, I remember thanking God for getting me through another year. I remember one day I was talking to one of the other nurses and thanking God for getting me through my divorce and she commented, "Oh that's what was wrong. You looked really angry. You didn't say anything." I said really, I was angry, I was hurt, and I wasn't putting on a mask. You know, and you know we talk about mask and what it looks like, and how we hide ourselves. One of the preachers I hadn't seen for a while when I was married, and when I went to this fashion show and when I saw them and this pastor said, "How are you?" And I said, "I'm fine." And he said, "No really, how are you?" And before I knew it I said, "I will bless the Lord at all time and his praise will continually be in my mouth." That shocked me. My soul was okay, but it was my flesh that wasn't okay. And I said that to say that I don't think that's fake. I don't know why people say that. And I imagine there have been times when I wore masks, but the mask is not the truth. But the trust—this is how I felt and wanted to look today and that is not a mask or being deceptive.

Tanya: I think a mask is when you're not being real with yourself, with what you're feeling, trying to pretend when you put the makeup and act like you are not dealing with the awareness of what you are going through and you put a mask on to deceive.

Researcher: Do you think black women have to wear a mask to survive?

Karen: Yes, but I also hear two questions being discussed? The first is what is fake and the second is masking. And for me, fake is where you personally allow yourself to interact with situations, persons that is against your moral fiber. It's like you are not being real. Like, I could be around a drug dealer cause they doing what's necessary to take care of business. But someone who is around a person to get something from that person and then go talk about them, to me that's fake.

A mask for me? I believe that we all wear from time to time. I know there are certain aspects of Karen that I allow myself with my girlfriends, so that's a different mask. When I'm at work with a group of people, I can be professional and articulate and that is a mask for that space. And they are all a part of me and who I am. There is a mask I wear with my supervisor cause she don't need to know the other parts of me. She is not privy to the sacred Karen that I may be with friends and family or in my worship. So there are masks we have to wear that are not so much negative but necessary to survive. They are needed for survival. For me there is another person, beside God, who I am able to be completely naked and vulnerable with, and that is my best friend, Jason. He has known me since I can remember. I am able to trust him cause he has shown me I can trust him. So I never have to wear a mask with him. So when we are not wearing a mask, that is sacred for me cause we can just be ourselves without judgment in safety.

Diane: There are various reasons we need to protect ourselves, but mostly because as African Americans and women we have been hurt. So we have issues with safety, trust, and may be insecure. For me, it's a work in progress. For me, its trust. My husband had to work really hard to where I took off my mask for him. And because we have been hurt so much, we need to wear mask to survive. There is still hurt, but I'm working through it.

Abbie: I also consider can I handle being naked and transparent before another. With all my isms and schisms and whatever the cause may be. As I was listening to Karen and everybody about a mask, I had to look it up as we expressed and shared our feelings cause it could seem like it seem negative cause it said to disguise, cover up, and deceive. I don't like the term mask cause of that, cause I see it more as when I was a nurse and we wore masks for protection. Protecting yourself from danger, harm, and infection, and we need to protect ourselves.

Tanya: Disguise. Well, maybe we can look at it that way, cause everybody is not worth us taking off our mask. And so maybe we have to disguise.

Abbie: So we not being deceptive. We are being protective.

Tanya: Let's try this on for size. There are various types of masks and we, I don't have to limit what those masks are. And what they're used for, that actually brings a deeper level of Tanya—versatility. Cause there were masks used for ceremonial, these mask were of deep spiritual meaning. I mean, so being able to be free. And so if I had been crying all night and put my mask on to go to class, then I feel free to do so.

Karen: I think its wisdom. If I'm in an important meeting, I'm not going to be speaking Ebonics. Howard Thurman wrote about meeting people where they are and Chaka Chan said, "I'm every woman," so I'm pre-packing myself, cause I know my crowd.

7. If you identify with the strong black woman image, do you feel you are always strong/always have to be strong?

Tanya: Being a strong black woman was part of surviving. All this stuff to deal with—school, work, kids, and so much more. Really you had to be everything and do everything. For me it was made clear early on when I first got pregnant with my son. I would have to continue to be expected to do everything that I had previously done. So for me, it's been a constant drive. First as a single mom, cause it's all or nothing. Then marriage. You got all that, in addition to being a mom. It was only survival. It has been a constant flow for me. I had to find some level of accomplishment. And the guilt of not listening to my mom on top of that. So for me the strong black woman has been a survival mode, not a martyr. But because I had to be. And I'd rather just do, because I had no choice not to do. I had a friend tell me, "You a strong black woman. You don't want no man to take care of you." And I said, "You shitting me? Yes I do." Being a strong black woman—the image and the continued going or pressing—is not because you want to but because you have to. I had to work two jobs and go to school. I had no choice if I was going to survive. And I think that the idea, because we have done it on our own, society puts black women in this category. But no, we had to do it on our own. We had no help. It's about survival.

Karen: Being a strong black woman is like playing football. When you get hurt or injured you get back up and keep moving. You can't let your injuries stop you. Also, in being able to talk about what it meant or represented for me to be a strong black women in this process has been helpful and I thank each of you for allowing me the space to do that. It was in your sharing, as well, and providing your story that helped me to share my story. This sacred space allowed me to share my story and listen to your stories.

Olivia: Being a strong black woman is survivor. I had to do what I needed to take care of my son—clean houses, sew people clothes, sell dinners, and whatever else I had to do to make sure he would be taken care of.

Abbie: I see myself as a strong black woman because I have always had to do what was needed in order for me to survive. No one took care of Abbie. I had to take care of myself.

Karen: A strong black or African American female has been a necessity for black women in this society. It was necessary in order to survive. It was something that needed to be done. Black women have always had to hold it down and care for everyone else while neglecting herself and her needs. The power to give voice is the greatest thing I can take with me. I take the mirror, the mirror to see myself even though my face may be washed with tears. And so at the end of the day to be a strong black woman is the person who I am and everything that has happened to me. It's all a part of the strong black women. Embracing the positive and the negative. When I leave, I will embrace my whole self. So I'm appreciative of everyone and what they have brought to the table. It's hard to say that without them and the group there would have been a part lacking.

Dianne: I can see similarities in our stories as we have all experienced pain, hurt, and some form of oppression, violence, and identify as strong black women. As a strong black woman, I realize God has me here for a reason. Firstly to be who I be; I don't want to change me for nothing. Secondly,

I am here as a vessel for God to encourage others. I personally do feel broken at times, but I have enjoyed the support of my sisters. I guess what I most struggle with is being uncomfortable in my skin and not being able to give my husband a baby. I'm not sure if God is punishing me for having an abortion early on in my life. I keep busy and make myself available to help others, even if I don't want to. For me also is that we as strong black women have our individual stories. But as a unified body we share some of the same stories that are on an individualistic side. For me personally, I have been able to hear and adhere to the times when I need to deal with the spirituality of God because I have to come face to face with my spiritual issues and that the image of the strong black women that sometimes gets in the way.

8. Have you ever been sexually abused or exploited?

When we arrived at the sixth session the women were able to talk openly about their experiences of rape, molestation, sexual abuse, and/or sexual exploitation. For many of them it was the first time that they had shared. Two of the women were molested by family members, one was sexually harassed by a neighbor, two experienced being raped, and one was almost raped. Each woman shared long narratives to take us through their experience and they worked out their feelings and thoughts as it relates to their experience of sexual violation. As the therapist, I served as a safe container, demonstrating that I was able to hold what they had to share. These are their experiences.

Karen: I'll start. I think for me it's been—I wouldn't say a struggle—but an interesting journey. I was molested from the time I was about five until age seven by relatives—more than one. And I have never told my parents. And the fact that I had to carry that with me has been difficult. And when I was ready to tell my parents, I didn't cause you know they were the ones who took me in and what would it do to my family and the ones who did it—and what would it do to me because they took me in and couldn't protect me or didn't know that they needed to protect me. The experience hindered me building relationships. It created a delay in that aspect and even in my adult life it's still difficult to build male/female relationships.

When I was thirteen I was raped and it was like wow. Okay. Then you think to yourself, okay. Are you a mark on you? Is there something wrong with you? cause this has happened to you. And why you? And then I said, "You know what I didn't tell anyone when I was younger." So after the rape,

I told someone and was told not to say anything and was threatened to be quiet. So then I told my girlfriend and she said, "You know you wanted it cause if you didn't you wouldn't have been there and it would have not happened." So I'm like, "Well dog. I'm telling you, that's not what happened." But if she saying that to me and she my friend, what is somebody else going to say to me? So let me not even deal with it. And I left it where it was and never dealt with that either.

Diane: For me, I was twelve and my middle brother and older brother decided to stay with their father. They lived with their dad when they were younger. Then my middle brother moved to Illinois with us when my mom was stationed at Fort Sam. One day she was at work. I don't even know how it began. But of course being the baby sister, you know that was my middle brother, you know he takes care of me, so I didn't think anything cause it must have been okay. I finally broke down and told my mom in 2009 and you know sometimes mothers have a sense of knowing, but they just don't know exactly what it is. She told me she kinda knew that something had probably happened but she just couldn't figure out what it was exactly. And she was telling me that and I struggle with this from the time before I told her because it stayed on mind. I was like, is this real? Did this really happen or am I making this up?

When I met my husband, and I told my husband I don't know if this will make you hate me but I need to let you know something about me. I was molested by my middle brother when I was twelve. But he didn't hate me. He comforted me and told me to tell my mother. He also encouraged me to forgive my brother and confront him with my memory of what happened. I was like, you serious? And he was like, yes you need to forgive your brother. This is the brother who has moved multiple times, been married multiple times, has four children by three different baby mothers. And when I finally told my mom on the advice of my husband, she said the same thing, which I need to tell him. And I said I don't know if I could do that. Why should I tell him? And she said to get it off of you. The next time both my brothers came down, I was scared to death to do it, but I spoke to him in the room and I didn't close the door because I was scared. I told him when we were little, do you remember when you raped me? And I don't know where his mind was, but he chose not to remember and to block it out. "I don't know," he said. And I said, "Regardless if you remember or not, it's something that happened that you did to me and I remember it very well and I just want you to know that I forgive you."

My mom told me that he was spoiled when she was pregnant with me and always put his hand on her stomach and when I was born he wanted her to give me back. And when I was older, he left me in the bathroom with the water running in the bathtub and he cut my hair. I don't know if he was being jealous or if he didn't particularly care for me. As for me, it was very hard, it was really, emotionally. And when he left out of the room I felt empty like it really didn't matter to him. I was like, I can't believe I haven't got help for this cause I probably need to. It still hurts.

The downside of this is that I had become sexually active shortly after, not sure if it is because of this, but I was about thirteen and was very sexually active. I was pregnant shortly after, but I got an abortion. My mom made me [weeping]. She never discussed it with me, which made me very angry. But that didn't stop the activity. Maybe six years later I became pregnant for a second time, but this time I gave the baby up for adoption because I was nineteen and I felt that I was gonna be focused on going to school. After that I learned about birth control and then I got protection. When I got married, I shared these things to my husband and I let him know about the abortion and the baby that I gave up for adoption. He didn't cast me out, and I praise God for that. One thing that I learned from my husband is that he loves me.

When I was in college, I remember that my neighbor tried to rape me. He tried to push his way in, and I said no, and he pushed the door and slap me back to the ground so hard my face was red. I said, "If you don't get out of here I'm going to have to call the police." And he said, "Go ahead and do whenever you want cause I'm going to have you tonight." I said "No, no you are not going to have me tonight." And I dialed 911. When they came and saw me on the floor they went to look for him and they found him in the neighborhood. To this day I remember how scared I was cause he knew where my church was and he could follow me around or go to church to get me. So it made me kinda of scared.

Researcher: Are there other feelings that come up for you after sharing?

Diane: Yeah, I guess the pain that I want to give my husband a baby and maybe

God is punishing me for the abortion and giving my baby away.

Researcher: Why do you believe God is punishing you? Where does that come from?

Diane: It comes from the church. That is something that I continue to wrestle with daily and I will continue to reflect on. I'm thankful because I'm able to express myself to God and my husband about my concerns.

Tanya: For me, I remember having a conversation with my brother who is about four years older than me. He was about twelve and I was about eight. And I remember him saying let me see yours and I will show you mine. And I remember my mom walked in and saw and flipped out. I don't know if she walked by and heard him, but she flipped. She let him have it. I also remember him always wanting to kiss me on my mouth and I didn't want to let anyone kiss me on my mouth. And I remember this picture with him trying to kiss me on my mouth and in the picture I was like, no. But I thank God to this day that my mom wouldn't let me go places and spend the night even at my cousin's house. I didn't understand it then but my grandmother gave my mom some insights about me and who I was going to be and to keep me away from certain family members. I remember older cousins and uncles saying things like, "If you wasn't family, if you wasn't my cousin/niece."

But my most traumatic memory was when my daddy got sick [teary eyes]. That was traumatic, for when his dementia set in and as time progressed during the last six months of his life he would grab my boobs and it got to the point where I would not want to see him or stand in front of him. The nurse also complained about his behavior and my mom would say, "Well, it's the dementia." So I didn't say anything to my mom about my daddy grabbing me. But it messed with my mind so much that I didn't want to go around him and finally I told my mom that daddy acts weird—maybe he thinks I'm you. And so my mom is a nurse and she gave me the medical breakdown of what was going on and told me what I shouldn't think because I know how he has always been with me before he got sick and I thought to myself bullshit. You shittin' me? It's my daddy sitting in that chair and it's my daddy who keeps reaching for my boobs. When I walk in the room he would say hi to me and ask for the kids so he knew it was me.

He had become so sexual, even with the nurses. It seemed like it was a pathological thing. It didn't seem like he just didn't know what he was doing. I talked to daddy about it and his eyes would just tear up cause he knew he tried me like a free sample. Or if he was even able to process what I said he was never able to answer what his tears was. And my mom would say, "Your daddy didn't do that." And I didn't know how to categorize that and that bit with my brother. My mom swooped in and saved me from danger so to speak. But my daddy, that was just an unmemorable right before he died. I remember I couldn't sleep and I was having a hard time trying to resolve it, so I focused on the relationship we had most of my life and chalked it up to what my mom had told me about dementia. I think in her way of dealing with it she dismissed it in some degree not to indulge.

Researcher: And how did that make you feel?

Tanya: It made me sad, but I wasn't going to let the last few months of his life dictate the previous part of our relationship. Me and my dad where close and we had a good relationship. He was my daddy and had never did anything like that before.

Erica: For me there are some things I don't remember and I think it's better not to remember. Some things that have come up for me since I've been here in the group as you have shared your experiences of sexual abuse is my grandson. My grandson was sexually molested by two different people, and one of the persons attempted it with his little sister so it made me start looking at things with my family.

I remember when I was twelve, I took a job working in the cleaners. The owner of the cleaners name was Nicholas King. He would routinely follow me around the store. I remember having to run and hide from him. I would just run because I liked my job. I was making $0.75 an hour placing tags on clothes. I wanted it so bad, but I finally reached a point where I had to quit because I was tired of trying to hide from him. I remember him doing all types of stuff with other girls in the back of his office. I quit because he was coming my way and I knew it, and so I couldn't tell my father because he would've tried to kill him and I think that that was the beginning with boys that shaped me.

I played with the girls for a minute and then I would go play with the boys. And so after a while people began to say, "Don't keep playing with the boys because it could turn dangerous." But I liked playing with the boys and when we played hide and seek we would kiss and touch and I'm not going to blame it on Nicholas King at the cleaners. But I know it had to do with that kind of lurking. And when I got to college, I would hear others tell their stories of molestation and touching and they too began to explore boys early as a result. But I lost my virginity in college. Before that, I would play around with boys but I would never go all the way.

The other night I was watching an episode of 20/20 where they talked about the girl that was sexually violated by football players. The story never said if they had sexual penetration but they penetrated her with objects.

That story brought up memories when I was in college. I went to a historical black college and lived off campus with some friends. It must have been my junior year cause by my senior year I had gotten saved. I had dated one of my boyfriends and we had just broken up. And he was an Omega. So we were at a party, me and my roommates. And one of my roommate's fiancé was also an Omega. And he was the drum major in the band and he was like a big brother to me.

At the party, people started to drink more and more, and started to watch pornography, and I was like, oh this is too much for me it's time to go because I was always between or trying to live between being really frisky and a prude and I was like, okay I'm not watching this. It was like ugly, nasty porn. And so I was sitting away from the TV and people watching the porn. And you know it was just a party, but I got drunk and I let this guy talk me into going into his room. I went into the bedroom with him and we were on the bed and I had my clothes off and before I knew it people started coming out of the woodwork. [Eyes watering] The closet, the closet door from the hallway, and I jumped up in the bed and it was kinda hard because it was a waterbed.

This guy had his roommates—four or five of them—come into the room as if I was going to agree to have sex with all of them. I was like, oh hell no. I started fighting them off of me and was screaming, "Someone get my big brother." He kicked them out and I put my clothes on and he walked me home and said, "Don't bring your ass around here no more." So I went to bed and I couldn't get it out of my head. It was six people that almost raped me, so I was upset [weeping]. I called my sister and it was the wrong thing to do because my sister, my brother, and cousin came to where I was and they made me go to the basketball game and show them who did it.

So my sister tried to talk me into reporting what happened, but I couldn't cause there were people at the school who knew my dad and had relationships with my family. [Weeping] I felt ashamed because I should not have been there. I should not have gone into his room, and I knew better. So I told them I was not going to report it and they left town. Unbeknownst to me, they got two of the guys.

I know that it was that experience that ran me back to God because after that experience it was hard to function. I went from functioning in school with a group of people to pretty much distancing myself from all of them. And that became a problem because they began to say, "So you think you too good for us." But I really just immersed myself in church. I would go to this Pentecostal church and this nondenominational church. I just did that until I graduated. One of the people who did that to me I was seeing all the time and he would try and talk to me. I didn't know if he was trying to apologize for what he did, but I refused to talk with him. So the next semester, I took an internship in my home city and then came back to graduate. I told myself that they didn't do anything, except the person I went into the room with. But I told myself all these reasons not to tell. We were off campus. We were in Mississippi. And over time I just put it out of my mind until I was teaching in Tuscaloosa.

My friend, Rose, came to live there with her husband, who was like my big brother who got me out of the room and I said, "I'm so glad you're here. Let's hang out." And the original guy, his roommate who invited his friends to have sex with me, started to visit all the time. But that brought back the memories of what happened. That kinda severed my relationship with her, and I just distanced myself and pulled away from them, and eventually I left Tuscaloosa.

Right before I came here, they were all going to a home game and was in a tragic accident and all of them were killed. I have really mixed emotions about all of them. [Weeping] I wanted to go to his funeral but I couldn't. I couldn't go to my big brother funeral. I called Rose and told her I was really sorry, but couldn't go the funeral but I would see her afterwards. I didn't want to go to the funeral with all of this, and two of the guys that died are the ones that my cousin and younger brother beat up. I had these really mixed emotions about the accident. At one point I was glad, and then I realized I had not forgiven them. Then I had to go through this process, they were dead. I would tighten up, then say to myself how stupid can I be to have let this happen to me? But just forgiving them was my biggest issue. I was just out of it.

I just began to fade away from the church and began to drink again. And then I drank and had sex with folk. I would just do that. I was not trying to have a relationship, and I think it affected my whole idea of trust to a level that I couldn't even think about until I got married. Then I got married again, and I think that, that taught me or led me to gravitate toward people I didn't trust. It was my second husband when I realized and said, "You proved me right. I knew you wasn't trustworthy." And I think that really has always been a big thing with me. I trust my family, and I grew up in a home where there was guns. My dad had a gun and my uncle, who was kinda like a mobster gangster, also had guns. And so I felt safe. I knew that they would protect me. But after that experience, I couldn't trust because I trusted him that if we were going to have sex it would just be me and him. I mean it's like, wow, they came out of the closet and when the door cracked open and the next thing I know I'm pushing them off me. I'm trying to throw my legs off the bed, and I'm thinking they thought this was going to be okay. And so that I just pushed it so far away, and once I got home I just continued to really push it away, really deep down.

Researcher: What feelings are coming up now?

Erica: Now I feel really sad and hurt. The sadness I think is cause I have never dealt with the pain of it. I have to deal with the remorse like because the way I felt when my brother, sister, and cousin came I was kinda angry because they came to distract me. I felt like when they died, I had not been given a chance to speak up for my rights. I should have just gone to [Capt. Sawyer] because he was my roommate's uncle. After [John Luther] died, I just felt remorse, sad, and I felt guilty, guilty because they died and guilty because it was my fault. That was my first feelings of guilt because I would say to myself, "You are not that stupid. Why would you even do that?" I was supposed to be street smart, the city girl from Detroit. I haven't been able to talk to my friends or no one like I'm talking and sharing in the group now because I felt like they would want me to be strong and they wouldn't be able to handle it. I never got the chance to say anything because I didn't have the courage.

Researcher: Is the remorse coming up because you were not able to confront them?

Erica: Yes, I think so. I always thought I would say something, but I never got the chance cause I didn't want to be seen as promiscuous or vulnerable. Out of the whole group, I was thought to be the one who would speak out. But when the time came, I could not go to the persons and say I don't like what you did to me.

Researcher: If they were here now what would you say to them?

Erica: I hate you for what you did to me. Hate is the first thing that came up for me, so I know I have a lot of work to do.

Researcher: If I were them I would say, "I'm sorry that I hurt you and caused you pain."

Erica: Thank you.

9. Do you ever have low self-esteem?

Erica: Don't feel like we deserve what we want cause our experience. The liberation is being able to ask for what you want and need, but your experience has kept you from asking. Remember for *Colored Girls*? Kimberley Elise need help but she didn't ask. Her self-esteem was affected by her experience of abuse from her husband and that is how it is for us—well I'll speak for myself, me. Also, Thandie Newton used her body in the movie cause she wasn't able to ask for help. Our experience of abuse impacts our self-esteem and we cope by causing more pain to ourselves, whether we are aware or not. To deal with my self-esteem or lack of, I tended to take on the role of helper. The helping role comes from being the youngest. It was a natural way to care for others, although sometimes it's not my place to help. When you have been violated and have not dealt with the pain or disappointments, helping others, giving to others—I guess in someone way was giving to me what I needed.

Researcher: And what was it that you needed and you didn't get?

Erica: I don't know. I guess acceptance. I felt accepted by my family but my home life was the opposite of what I faced when I left home to go into society. I think that is why I opted to work for black companies and institutions, cause I wasn't accepted in the white world. It made me feel fragmented.

Researcher: Tell us what fragmented means to you?

Erica: It's like being broken in pieces and so it's hard to know who you are cause all the pieces either are broken or don't fit.

Karen: As I sat here and listen and unpacked my life it hasn't been great. My mom was pregnant at seventeen and my dad was murdered when I was eleven months old. My mom gave me to her older sister to raise, and so I have two families. On top of that being, raped and molested. Although my experience has really impacted me. And my other friend who experienced sexual abuse, when I tried to talk to her, she says it happens to everybody and doesn't want to talk about it. I don't know the specifics of what happened to her, but she shuts down completely and doesn't want to talk about it. I be like, what is going on? And had all my girlfriends gone through this experience and why can't we just talk about it out in the open so we can deal with it, at least some of this stuff.

I've learned during my rape crisis experience from my clinical supervision that the highest rate of molestations happen within the family. And so when you talk about reporting rape and things like that, molestation is more so coming from the family and is not going to be reported quickly or at all because of family dynamics. Because if you report it, then you breaking up the family. So if you report that daddy molested you the mom gonna be like, no because then my husband going to jail. And so the children continue to be abused. Because they don't talk. And if it bothers them they don't talk either because you could be at a family reunion and the one who molested or raped you is sitting across the table joking like nothing happened. So we don't talk about it. And when you act out drinking or hypersexual you may be getting HIV-infected because this behavior of promiscuity causes bad behaviors.

Then your life is hindered more and when you find the courage to tell what happened. The response is quit lying and he didn't do that to you, you just a lie, you just like your mama. It's like, really? So what do you do with that? We turn it inward. So for me, I gained 200 pounds because of that, you know what I'm saying? Not because I wanted to be a big girl because I was always a size 5 or 6. I think I was a size 12, which was my biggest when I was in high school. So I wouldn't date. And so I ate and I ate like nobody's business. So of course my self-esteem was effected. Eating was my comfort that made me feel comfortable. I got used to that and then I had my boyfriend on a Friday night when I got of age and realized I should have had a real boyfriend cause he wasn't really my boyfriend. He was just someone that I would have sex with.

And when I was around twenty-one or twenty-two years of age, I wasn't dating anybody. It's not like I wasn't having sex because I was. I was very promiscuous, but I didn't understand then what I know now. I couldn't stop that behavior cause I didn't realize I could have control over my body until I was twenty-three years old. I moved here to Atlanta and that is when I realized how to control my body. I had to gain control of myself and figure out who I was—and my friends judged me but they would never talk to me to figure out what was going on inside of me. One of my girlfriends I could never tell because she was like non-supportive because when I was raped at thirteen she said I wanted it, that's why I was raped.

Researcher: Thank you for sharing. How did it make you feel to hear your friend say that?

Karen: I mean, really? So I never really trusted her. It may have impacted me from trusting others, too. I mean we still friends, but for me, I had to try and find out ways to learn more about me. I mean, really. Until right now, I'm just getting a grip about me and what I want to deal with, and then losing weight has taken an emotional toll on me. Just a lot of emotional stuff, so I would stuff my feelings and I'm just realizing that. I even lost 100 pounds and was working on myself, and enjoyed going to the gym every day and eating right when I came to ITC. I was like I just started all over again, and it was intense.

Researcher: I want to affirm you for not giving up. Can you share what has helped you get to the place you are today?

Karen: My relationship with God and coming to ITC helped because it helped bring a spiritual aspect into my experience, and education has been a way of coping from me. I needed to start living again so doing my CPE, being at Grady, all of that has purpose in helping me process. Also, the group, being able to talk about my experience. And hopefully I'll get it right because I want to settle down and have some type of stability. In Atlanta, I have found safety because when I go back home to California I can't be there long because I have to hold on to these trees full of secrets. And so then I'm stressed. Staying away is not the healthiest coping mechanism, but it has helped me this far.

Researcher: I want to encourage you to continue to use your voice and honor your experience and stay on your journey towards healing.

Tanya: When people look at me, they think that I have no worries. But I do struggle with my self-esteem. I mean really, growing up I was ugly and now you want to tell me I'm beautiful. How am I supposed to embrace that now?

Reflective Journaling

Abbie: "What does it mean to be an angry black woman?" When I was in the third grade, my teacher walked over to me and said that I was never going to be anything. . . . I didn't even tell my mother what happened. . . . I was ashamed and since then I have been trying to please people. . . . I guess it's cause I'm dark with a big nose and mouth. . . . I looked different from my family. "Can I handle being naked in front of another with all my schisms" I am a fifty-nine year old, African American woman who has always struggled with insecurity, doubts, and fears. I am learning how to be me, but it is difficult.

I'm struggling to be me. I continue to bump into myself. Can I afford to be risky and discover myself? I have always been afraid to share my thoughts with others. I would express my opinion and wonder what the other person would be thinking after I shared. I always found myself wondering why a person would be interested in me. I was not an attractive and interesting person. I have not liked myself for a very long time. I thought I was not important or good enough and always thought that everybody could see inside of me. I always tried to make everyone happy and I needed them to affirm me, no matter what. I always second guessed myself. Needing the affirmation of others made me angry growing up. I would argue with myself in my head because of the way people treated me, but I would never voice how I felt, even today. How could I be important to others when I wasn't important to myself? I always looked at the angry black woman as something bad. I never really thought about why I was angry and how my anger keeps me isolated.

My feelings of inadequacy caused me to isolate myself because I didn't feel like I fit in. If I wasn't accepted by my family, how could I be accepted by others? I used to laugh when people would talk about black women are always angry. But know I don't find it funny. I don't really know who I am. Growing up, I was always teased because of my dark complexion, hair texture, and features. I am trying to come to terms with why I sought silence and isolation instead of my parents. I struggle with why they didn't help me. Why have I suffered all this time struggling with my identity and still suffering today? The group has made a difference. I am open to explore who I am, although it's difficult. The group help provide me support to take the risk.

Olivia: "Sticks and stones may break my bones—our identity is formed by our surroundings wounded and hurt." I don't know why people getting on band wagon now wanting to be called African Americans. On my birth certificate it says colored. I identify myself as an American Christian woman. "Staying busy keeps me from being angry."

I am sixty-two, and I have an adult son. I am divorced from my husband who was a preacher and a ho. I was raised Baptist, but didn't agree with how they treated women. And after the abuse of my husband, I joined the Presbyterian Church where I am an ordained elder. I'm not going to identify with something now because it's popular. I identify as a Christian.

Journaling is difficult because it brings up unpleasant feelings—feeling overwhelmed. Reflecting on who am I? Feelings of rejection by my sisters. Feeling like no one will be there for me and it hurts. My mom taught us to be strong women. But I'm tired of being dumped on and being different from my sisters and other women who talk about me because I'm not stuck on all the designer clothes and things. I was raised by both of my parents. Do I state what I need? No. When I voice how I feel it makes people uncomfortable. Now I am working on making simple statements with authority. I'll just be hard and cold so I won't break.

Thinking about doing what is right versus doing what is wrong. How do I find balance? I need to take care of myself because I have no one to rescue me. It's just me. I'm going to be driven to take care of myself. My family won't help because I left what they called a perfect marriage. Although we had money, he didn't treat me right. He abused me. I'm working on letting go and learning what is on the inside of me. My mom was a strong woman and made the decisions in the household, and my dad was the disciplinary. I am just learning about saying no. It's difficult, though, to say no still, and I say yes until it hurts. I go out of my way for other people, but they have not done the same for me. I feel alone and lonely. I'm working on learning how to express my anger. I won't cry though. Black women don't have a voice. We must fit into other's culture.

Reflecting, I think my mom internalized a lot of stuff looking back. Taking care of myself has not been an option as a divorced, single mom. I choose to put my son's welfare first. I was in survival mode and left a marriage of convenience and financial wealth because his abuse and oppression. And the oppression of his mother became too much to bear, in addition to his cheating. I have been struggling with what is on the core of myself. My identity and the perception of myself to others. Wondering who will cry for the little girl. I'm feeling perplexed. What does oppression mean to me? It is weighted down by society and unable to get what you are qualified for—continuously being rejected. I have been reflecting on taking off the mask and the need for the mask is survival—is it safe to take off the mask? Do I have the right to keep my mask on? I believe that God is the only safe place that I can take off my mask. He has been my steady companion and strength. I will continue to work on unraveling my feelings toward my identity, explore being busy and my feelings of abandonment, loneliness, rejection, anger, and desire to isolate.

Dianne: "Giving up is not an option." "I don't know who I am." "I am here as a vessel for God to encourage others." Transition has always been a part of my life. I didn't always embrace it, but I can honestly say it's necessary. I am forty-six, an AME pastor of two churches, wife, and doctoral student (I should be graduating May 2016), and a teacher's assistant. At the age of twenty-three my life changed when I was diagnosed with multiple sclerosis. What I find myself reflecting on is identity and what is beauty? As a light-skinned woman, I must admit that I didn't experience color barriers growing up. I lived a sheltered life and my parents were in the military. I guess for the most part what has kept me going is my relationship with God, wanting to please God, and be who he created me to be. I listened to the other stories of the women and the struggles they faced as a result of their skin color, and it hurts me. But I can see similarities in our stories as we have all experienced pain, hurt, and some form of oppression, violence, and identify as strong black women.

Finding balance is a challenge for me. My schedule is busy and I'm learning how to stop and look at myself to take care of myself. Resting is very important to me although difficult. Prayer is what helps to get me through. As a strong black woman, I realize God has me here for a reason. Firstly, to be who I be; I don't want to change me for nothing. Secondly, I am here as a vessel for God to encourage others. I personally do feel broken at times, but I have enjoyed the support of my sisters and look forward to a relationship outside of group. I guess what I most struggle with is being uncomfortable in my skin and not being able to give my husband a baby. I'm not sure if God is punishing me for having an abortion early on in my life or giving a baby up for adoption. But it's the constant pain that I have. I keep busy and make myself available to help others even if I don't want to.

Reflecting on the statement "be who you be," made by Karen—what do you do if you don't know who you are? I mean really. What are you to do when you was never asked or it just wasn't important to others and now you find yourself struggling to identify with you are you. I think that is a question that honestly is going to take some time. I will pray and seek God for help cause he always helps. I have enjoyed the group and talking with other sisters and I will be taking away self-care—making time for myself, resting, pampering, meditation, and continuing to define who I am. It's hard saying good-bye.

Karen: "As African American women we have so many stereotypes and stigmas out there about who we are, what we need, and what we stand for." I am forty-eight, single, in a relationship with no children. I am on track to being a chaplain in the COGIC church. This process group happened to take place during my first semester of clinical pastoral education. At times the process of this group conflicted with the steps I'm taking in my personal journey with CPE. I don't want to bring up all the bad and negative memories that happened to me during my childhood. I'm an adult now. I have considered leaving the group so I could really focus on what I should be getting from my verbatim groups. My boyfriend, who is my support system, has encouraged me to stop attending the group mainly because the issues that I've had to face regarding my history of being sexually abused opened up a door that has been nailed shut.

My boyfriend has been part of my life since I was five years old and has been so supportive of me. So when he encouraged me to walk away from the group, I considered it, but remained with it to complete this process. Reflecting on how I identify myself and my journey, well I'm a compassionate African American woman who is a product of unwed teen parents. I was raised by my maternal aunt and her husband. I have earned five college degrees and preparing to complete a doctorate of ministry program starting in the fall of 2015. I can honestly say that I haven't always liked myself, especially when I measured myself according to the judgments of others. Over the last fifteen years or so, I can honestly say that I love me and appreciate my own company. God has shown me that all that I ever needed is already within me and that I am responsible for the quality of my life and for my own happiness. I trust God for all that I am. I love my personality and my openness to embracing and loving others for who they are. I have a big heart and have realized that I have taken responsibilities for others until I have disabled them from doing for themselves. I have learned to refrain from such behavior, for it is self-defeating. The more I do for others the less they do for themselves.

I am thankful for this group and appreciative of the opportunity to work through, or at least begin to work through, the process of addressing certain issues that have followed me all of my life. Now is the time for me to shed that baggage and to move towards a healthier life. Owe that to myself. In order for me to be all that God called me to be, I have to remain focused on God's will and trust God through all of my trials and tribulations.

Erica: "Others see me as a strong black woman." Fifty-five years of age, divorced twice, separated now—but we are talking about getting back together. I guess I'm not sure if it has something to do with him being sick. I have two adult sons and I suffer from sleep apnea. I am a proud grandmother of a granddaughter named Cecilia, and I was raised by both parents who are still together. I have two older sisters and a younger brother, and I am an elder in AME church. I have a non-profit business and work with families back home. I have several degrees and have held various positions in academia and lived all over.

I grew up in home that was very Afrocentric. My father was a professor and my mother was a teacher. I don't really identify as a strong black women. Others see me as a strong black woman. I don't think we can be strong all the time. I believe we have been and are resilient, and the strong black woman is a name that has been projected on us by society. Growing up, my dad taught us to have pride in our ethnicity.

Reflecting on myself, I'm struggling now to decide if I should take my husband back. I learned that he is sick and I feel like I should be there to take care of him. I'm looking forward to graduating in May. Also thinking about me giving until it hurts. I think it may be because that is the role I played being the youngest, I guess. It's been natural wanting to do and care for others, although sometimes it's not my place to help cause it might not be helpful. I think that the experience from when we were younger, we didn't have the words especially when you have been violated and have to deal with the pain, and so in order not to experience disappointment, I give, do, or care for.

Tanya: "Everybody is not worth my nakedness." "There are various types of me. I don't have to limit what those masks are and what and when I use the masks for . . . they bring different levels of myself." 2012 answered the call to ministry. Forty-one, divorced twice, an adult son, teen age daughter, and a granddaughter. I was raised by both parents. I recently lost my dad, which has been very difficult. We were very close. I was closer to my dad then my mom. As I reflect on abuse, I ask myself: Am I so emotionally removed that I have forgotten? Whose identity do I take on? What do I see when I see me? I feel grateful. Stop and think—real feelings—real healing. What do I need? Do I really need anything now? I feel so lost without him. Why can't I have my own? It's been almost ten years since a "real" relationship.

Nothing ever "fit." Then . . . BAM! There he is! Engaged and all! Really? Okay, so he's not married. So he's still game right not! I should have known better. First, I shouldn't allow myself to be so needy and second a commitment is just that—a commitment! Nothing seems to make sense. . . . Nothing feels right. I can't focus. . . . I can't concentrate. I cry compulsively. I recognize the signs. . . . I don't wanna fall into a slump without the strength to climb out. I'm feeling pretty weak. Why did he have to be so wonderful? So now what? How do I walk away from this un-fractured? How do I believe that I'm not being rejected? How do I know that this won't draw me ever further "within"?

I just heard a song on Pandora that distinctly reminded me of a specific time in my past. . . . However, it is also a minor image of my present. "Love." Keysha Cole. I keep thinking, "love" is gonna have my back!!! At least this time. . . . But man, I'm wrong this time!!! What is it about ME that I keep attracting this? So, all of these talks about colorism . . . she happens to be very light skinned. My son's father married a biracial woman, my ex-husband—both of them pissed me off and pursued and later married light-skinned and Caucasian women. So why not me? Why does it seem I keep losing to the lighter ladies? Why do I not ever recognize it? What kind of healing do I need? Can I really expect to be or have what I want? What kind of healing has to happen? What would it mean to write it down for Myrna to read? . . . It would mean allowing transparency. Documented delirium! That's what it would mean.

How much of me do I want others to know? How much of me do I want Myrna to know? Many of the incidents that I would avoid writing about are around shame and guilt. There are some things in my life that I would rather nobody except God know about. I think this goes back to discretion versus deception. These past two months have been such an emotional roller coaster. It's like been bathing in the "dumbs" all month long! Perhaps the consistent unearthing or deep-seeded issues has taken its toll. I can't wait until spring break! I just need not think anymore.

The "dark girls" conversation has surfaced again! What does healing look like? Someone stated that when we no longer recognize color, then well experience healing. I disagree. . . . When we don't see color, we're just uncoordinated mix/matched people. However, when we see color, it's how that acknowledgment affects that indicates progress, growth, and healing. I'm going to continue to wrestle with me. Explore my feelings and deal with my anger. I want to be naked, but can I allow myself to be naked?

Good-Bye Wrap-up Session

At the termination session, we explored the process of saying good-bye and what that represented for the women. Out of the six participants, four struggled with good-bye and two acknowledged they have worked on saying good-bye in the past. Out of the six women, two will be graduating and transitioning into their ministry and context, and saying good-bye to this academic career, Georgia, and friends during their seminary journey. To close out, we reflected on four questions.

1. Reflecting on the group process can you share what you learned?

Olivia: I have learned the ability to trust women again. After feeling like the odd one out—the different one—like I have been my whole life with my family and sisters, this experience has shown me that I am able to trust women and be in relationship with women and feel safe and not alone. This has been a good experience and I'm looking forward to building upon my relationship with these women.

Diane: What can I say? This has been a life-changing experience for me? I have learned the importance of rest and self-care. Putting my needs first and not being busy—to be busy. I learned that my business was to avoid me because I didn't like myself and I didn't want to be alone with myself. Being still allowed me to deal with my pain of sexual abuse by my brother. I'm learning how to breathe and just be, allowing myself the time I need to explore my feelings and take one day at a time.

Tanya: I'm learning me. Who I am? What I want. As I deal with the pain of being by myself and struggling with my identity as a black women. Dealing with my masks and why I need them. And being uncomfortable as I be.

Abbie: First, I want to say thank you for creating this space where I can wrestle with myself. I learned that I don't have to seek affirmation from everybody—that I have to spend time with Abbie and love Abbie and stop running from myself. I'm learning how to let go of the pain and rejection that I struggle with of feeling like I have to be what everyone else wants when I don't know what I want or who I am and I'm okay with that. I guess I'm learning how to be comfortable with being uncomfortable if that makes sense.

Karen: I have learned that I have dealt with the pain from my sexual abuse and my work in this group has demonstrated a confirmation, if you will, that I have been able to reframe my story. I don't feel the stuff that used to come up when I talked about my story in the past, and so for me, the ability to reframe my story. There is no more revocation for that story and I'm okay with that. So I don't need to tell that story—but now I have the opportunity to tell a different story, one that includes healings.

I'm appreciative of the group because of what the circle represented for me and allowing me to share my story in safe space, and it was timely as I am also in the midst of my own CPE and was ready to explore, examine, and find healing and peace. Also, in being able to talk about what it meant or represented for me to be a strong black women in this process has been helpful and I thank each of you for allowing me the space to do that. It was in your sharing, as well, and providing your story that helped me to share my story. This sacred space allowed me to share my story and listen to your stories. This process enabled me to confirm that my previous story doesn't define me and I'm going to continue to work on Karen and own my stuff and that okay. I'm embracing me, for a change, and my needs, and not worrying about everyone else's needs.

Erica: I'm learning how to let go. I didn't realize how much I was holding onto from the past, and I know that this is just the beginning. So let go.

2. What will you take with you?

Tanya: I will take with me what I felt in this space, so I guess security. I will take away all that I have learned. Previously, I didn't socialize and interact, and what I recognized in this group how sheltered my life has been, and learning Tanya more and more, although scary and hurtful, it is necessary. And in this group I've learned more about who I really be and figuring it out as I go. This is also been timely in the sense that there was a situation from the beginning of the group. And examine and really felt what my worth was. And being in this group and discussing worth and self-worth, the mask, and so all the issues that I was dealing with and experiencing, affirmation and the truth of who we really are as truth about who we are not, who they say we are, but who we really are. This has been a truly beautiful experience.

Olivia: I'm going to have to say hope. Because of this experience I'm hopeful. I never thought that I would be able to be like this with other women because I was treated so bad and used by my sister and girlfriends. I'm also grateful to be able to say good-bye to the old Olivia and embrace the new Olivia. I walk away different and I glad to see the difference that I see in myself. And that is what I will take away with me as well.

Erica: Well, for me, I'm going to carry of piece of each of you—what I've learned from you. I leave here with a feeling of hope and joy cause the idea of sisterhood. I will treasure and cherish this experience and the good relationships that were developed. I see that in this group, that despite the reality, the truth of touch and support of each other is an awesome experience, and important, and it helps us to support one another. And I thank you for creating this environment. Grateful for the sharing and trusting in the space, and the sense that everyone will take away and have learned and experienced a sacredness. Our time in this group was well spent and I just say thank you to each of you.

Abbie: I'm just so grateful. I wish it didn't have to end. Friendship. You ladies have shown a side of women that I have not seen before. I didn't feel judged or that I had to second-guess myself. So friendship. You can see I'm getting tearful. So for me to cry and share is a good thing. Before, I used to think tears were weak and I didn't want people to see my cry. And now I am able to cry. And so learning to acknowledge my pain and discomfort, and the pain and discomforts of others, has been a great experience for me. So the experience of sharing and knowing that we are women of value. I will also take with me the power of affirmation—affirming myself and not waiting for others to confirm me. I take peace with me, and I appreciate the honesty and being around women who didn't mind sharing it helped me to see that I'm not the only one going through and that I'm not alone. The power to give voice is the greatest thing I can take with me. I take the mirror—the mirror to see myself even though my face may be washed with tears. And so at the end of the day, to be a strong black women is the person who I am, and everything that has happened to me it's all a part of the strong black woman. Embracing the positive and the negative—when I leave, I will embrace my whole self. So I'm appreciative of everyone and what they have brought to the table. It's hard to say that without them and the group there would have been a part lacking.

3. What would you have liked to discuss and/or changed?

Abbie: For me, I wish it was longer. There needs to be something like this on campus, or a place where women can just talk and deal with our stuff without being judged.

Olivia: I agree with Abbie. If it wasn't for this group, I would have never known how beautiful each of these women is. And now I'm about to graduate—you brought us together. Also, that it is possible to have relationships with black women and not feel judged or like, I don't belong.

Tanya: I agree with Olivia, this has been nice. Now that I feel more comfortable, it's over. But I wish you luck with your research. It's needed.

Karen: Um—what would I change? I don't think I would change anything, but I agree with Tanya that this research is needed. Just look at where we are meeting in the middle of a community that broken, in a seminary at a prime location for ministry, and we are not involved. I think what we explored in the group should lead us to real ministry and help the people who can't get what we getting—all this wisdom. One thing I would add is that there is a need for a space where broken black brothers can come and deal with their stuff. They had a failure to launch. They have been broken and abused by society, and so in relationship and embracing the strong, the black, it's because our black men are not present and when they want to be present, they are not able to. So it's a struggle—and for me I do want to be married by the pain of the broken black man who is in pain. I can walk with him but I can't bear his pain, and therefore needs a safe. And it's so sad because we don't process together. It would be nice if we could discuss and go through together to provide understanding between the black man and black woman.

Diane: Well for me, I agree with everyone. And as a pastor I think we need more groups like this. It would change how we as pastors hold things inside. We need an outlet to express our feelings and moments of depression and uncertainty. Although God is able to provide us the strength, I think that a group like this can impact women in ministry. For me, also, is that we as strong black women have our individual stories. But as a unified body we share some of the same stories that are on an individualistic side. For me personally, I have been able to hear and adhere to the times when I need to deal with the spirituality of God because I have to come face to face with my spiritual issues and that the image of the strong black women that sometimes get in the way. And piggy backing off of Karen, I agree—having no place for black men especially dealing with the strong black women, and me sharing with my husband that we are on the same team, and seeing others who feel like they are in competition and seeing the intimidation and insecurities. Also, I'm grateful to my sisters for sharing and being transparent. I'm hoping that as we leave this place and see each other outside of this space that we can embrace each other as true sisters and have genuine concern for one another.

Erica: I agree with everything that was said. I wouldn't change anything, but I want to add that we need something like this for our brothers.

4. In a sentence, or using one word, answer the question "Who am I?"

Karen: I am a survivor. *Tanya*: I am worthy. *Erica*: I am empowered. *Abbie*: I am confident. *Dianne*: I am enough. *Olivia*: I am valued.

6

Psychological, Sociocultural, and Theological Themes / Theological Reflection / Discussion of Discourse

THIS CHAPTER IS DESIGNED to highlight the psychological, socio-cultural, theological themes, and theological reflection and discussion of discourse to explore the experience of the black women and the research data presented in the previous chapters. I will draw on self-psychology, womanist theology, and African-centered psychology.

Psychological Themes

Defects of the self occur mainly as the result of empathy failures from the side of the selfobjects [the parent/caregiver].

—HEINZE KOHUT, *THE RESTORATION OF SELF*

The aim of [self-psychology], as well as the ... curative function of all loving relationships, is the healing of the vertical split and the restoration of wholeness. This might be seen to correspond to the theological notion of the healing power of grace.

—PAMELA COOPER-WHITE, *MANY VOICES*

The psychological themes that developed from this research project, as outlined in the previous chapters, pertaining to the fragmentation of African American women and their distortion of self are depression, isolation, low self-esteem, identity, shame, rejection, abandonment, loneliness, anger, and fear. We will explore the development of these themes utilizing self-psychology. Kohut asserts that the failure of an environment to provide sufficient empathy could lead to a fragmentation of the self.[1] Further, he notes that a perspective of cure of the self occurs when the analyst is the selfobject and has the ability to provide an adequate empathic response. He writes:

> Because psychological health was formerly established through the solution of inner conflicts, cure, whether in a narrow or in a broad sense, was then seen exclusively in terms of conflict solution through the expansion of consciousness. Because psychological health is now achieved with ever-increasing frequency through the healing of a formerly fragmented self, cure, whether in a narrow or broad sense, must now also be evaluated in terms of achieving self-cohesion, particularly in terms of the restitution of the self with the aid of a re-established empathic closeness to responsive selfobjects.[2]

A Kohutian model of doing psychotherapy can be beneficial when working with African American women because it allows for their story to be shared through their lens, and for the counselor to demonstrate understanding and objectivity. This allows black women to gain a sense of voice and empowers them to tell their story in their own time. Kohut asserts, "The analyst will even have to realize that a patient whose childhood selfobjects has failed traumatically in this area will require long periods of "only" understanding."[3] Thus, Kohut's therapeutic technique of empathic attunement creates an opportunity for African American women to repair the break and distortion of self that created inner feelings of depression, isolation, low self-esteem, identity, shame, rejection, abandonment, loneliness, anger, and fear. Moreover, through an adequate response of empathy with the therapist as the selfobject, black women can move from a fractured self to a cohesive self.

Sociocultural Themes

God creates persons *imago Dei* (in God's image) in a manner that embraces diversity, mutuality, and wholeness.

—CHERYL KIRK-DUGGIN, *MISBEGOTTEN ANGUISH*

---

1. Kohut, *Restoration*, 76–77.
2. Kohut, *Restoration*, 76–77.
3. Kohut, *Restoration*, 88.

> Structural evil stereotypes of black womanhood... continue to have profound influence.... Aunt Jemima [the] property and commodity. Sapphire [the] coloredness, strong, and opinionated. Tragic Mulatta [the] empire and empire building [of the] unabashed creation of the white imagination ... light skinned ... mixed race. Welfare Queen [the image of] Black poverty and Mammy gone bad and Topsy [is the] black ... Pickaninny.
>
> —Emilie M. Townes, *Womanist Ethics*

> Racism corrupts the magnificent rainbow of humanity created by God.... [And when the] dominant culture signi[fies] that ... God is white ... then the question of being made in God's image becomes more crucial. In addition ... what does it mean to be human?
>
> —Cheryl Kirk-Duggin, *Misbegotten Anguish*

In this section I will explore cultural transference, cultural countertransference, and cultural selfobjects with regards to examining the themes of denial of personhood utilizing a womanist viewpoint. A womanist viewpoint of exploration is necessary as it "creates a way of seeing that is (1) eschatological or goal oriented, (2) about total health and liberation of individual and communal mind/soul, spirit, and body, (3) about the relational historical Black experience, (4) based on real feelings, experiences, actions, and (5) transformational life changing process that enhances everyone."[4]

To explore the concepts of cultural transference and cultural countertransference, I bring in the voices of clinicians Leslie C. Jackson and Beverly Greene. Jackson and Greene expand the scope of cultural transference as the "emotional reactions of a client to the therapist based on the client's sense of who the therapist is, culturally, with respect to race, ethnicity, religion, gender, age, social class, and other factors ... cultural transference looks beyond race to acknowledge other obvious differences between the client and the therapist, and it allows for 'cultural' reactions by a client to a therapist who is similar with respect to race and gender. [And] cultural countertransference as the therapist's emotional reactions to the client based on the client's race,

---

4. Kirk-Duggan, *Misbegotten Anguish*, 12.

ethnicity, religion, gender, age, social class, or the like ... [anything] that gets in the way of seeing the client more clearly.[5]

Jackson and Green go further, discussing the "real relationship" that occurs in the therapeutic space between the counselee and the pastoral counselor. The real relationship is the realistic relationship established between the counselee and the counselor and not one of fantasy. This is important when working with black women because there needs to be a genuine connection in order for the therapeutic alliance to be established, and for black women to become unarmored.

It was in the initial counseling session after greeting the women that Olivia asked to know my ethnicity. I asked what her thoughts were on my ethnicity. She replied, "I'm not sure." Waiting for my response, each woman in the session was rapt with attention, awaiting my response. I identified my ethnicity as African American. After my response, it appeared that the women trusted me a little more, and the anxiety that was present in the space seemed to lessen. My countertransference towards them was adult—elder, as the majority of them were old enough to be my mother. Recognizing this, we explored perceptions. It was in that first session that the women began to open up and began to discuss oppression and their experience of racism, sexism, and classism.

During another session, we discussed the issue of racism and explored more deeply as we dealt with colorism. That session was tense as Tanya was talking and going on about light skinned, long fine hair—you know the description of the tragic mullata. I asked, "How does it feel to sit in this space with me as the counselor as I fit the description of two shades lighter than a paper bag with fine long hair?" Tanya replied, "Today you caught me on a good day. But in the past, I would be pissed." I informed her that it would be okay if she was pissed, and she gazed at me as if that was the first time she had been given permission to be angry. In that moment a connection, a therapeutic alliance, was developed. The issue of colorism can be an unspoken theme in the therapeutic encounter, especially if the counselee is struggling with her identity and unresolved feelings regarding the color of her skin.

Sheppard explores the black women's self-esteem predicated on colorism, hair, and ideology. She highlights Williams's assertion that "black women's self-esteem is [also] undermined by the use of alien aesthetic criteria to assess black women's beauty and value."[6] Moreover Sheppard writes,

---

5. Jackson et al., *Psychotherapy African American*, 20, 24.
6. Sheppard, *Self, Culture*, 63.

"The exploitation of black women's bodies through enslavement, rape, forced pregnancy, and other forms of violence reverberates relationally and inter-generationally, and undergirds much of the tension and conflict related to colorism, dialogue related to hair, and black genealogy."[7] Tanya's examination of her and her mother's self-esteem comes not only from their dark skin, but their features, and hair texture, as well. As a result, they were rejected by members of their own and external community. Tanya shared the following in a session around the image of black women:

> Our identity is informed by our surroundings and when you hear words that are harmful how do you not allow it to affect you? cause words do have power, I mean everything to describe me by others from elementary to college were you black this and you black that, you big lip, you this and you that—all negative. I mean you black nerd, really. And then to have a classmate here say they are going to kill the white girl in me, and the comments about my hair. I mean really. Come on. When does it end? Am I supposed to see myself as beautiful when my own people and society has defined or deemed dark as ugly? Everything is about what I look like and nothing to do with my character. What we are called by others and what we allow others to call us, all of that shapes us and our identity. So this point of identity, who are we really if we have identified with those who don't see us or have defined us not in a positive way? And even though my mom tried to tell me I was beautiful, she continues to struggle with her own beauty as a result of how she was treated. And how long ago was that? And to this day she does not see herself as beautiful.

During the initial group session, and the sessions that followed, I was able to be the cultural needed for Tanya and others as, together, we worked through issues of identity, beauty, racism, sexism, classism, and other isms that hindered their narcissist needs from being met, and get to a place where we can work towards a vital change in the group and individually.[8] Kohut asserts two principal functions of cultural objects:

1. they embody cultural ideas that can provide moral uplift to cultural members, and

---

7. Sheppard, *Self, Culture*, 63.
8. Sheppard, *Self, Culture*, 114.

2. they constitute the collectivity of alter egos that populate the social environment—values, morals, etc.[9]

Spiritual and Religious Themes

Lastly, the *Clinical Manual of Cultural Psychiatry* explores the use of religion and spirituality among African American women, and the fundamental role it plays in the cultural context of their everyday life and how they cope. The beginning of the book reviews the changes to the Diagnostic and Statistical Manual of Mental Disorders-IV (DSM-5) and highlights the following for clinicians when making space for culture in the therapeutic treatment plan: (1) the cultural identity of the individual, (2) cultural conceptualizations of distress, (3) psychosocial stressors and cultural features of vulnerability and resilience, (4) cultural features (elements) of the relationship between the individual and the clinician, and (5) overall cultural assessment. The authors use this as a guide as they explore the implications of culture not only to engage the counselee but also not to misdiagnose.[10]

The research conducted by the American Psychiatric Association in the manual denotes the importance of culture in the therapeutic encounter. The authors write:

> Awareness of the patients' religious or spiritual beliefs and practices allows the therapist to accommodate such beliefs in the case formulation of the patient, including the patients struggle to find meaning, the patients meaning of relating to others, the effect of spiritual belief on the transference relationship between patient and therapist, and the therapist's capacity to make appropriate referrals when religion or spiritual questions extend beyond the therapist's expertise.... Therefore it is critical to access the patient's religious beliefs during the initial session because the patient may have a presence for a therapist who belongs to the same faith.[11]

The implication of the socio-cultural theme of personhood must not be denied because it makes space for the whole person to be present—seen in the image of God—and deconstructs the negative, stereotypical images of the black woman. It embraces her body, identity, and allows her to

---

9. Seeley, *Cultural Psychotherapy* 57.
10. Lim, *Cultural Psychiatry*, 417–118.
11. Lim, *Cultural Psychiatry*, 426.

reconstruct her story, for her voice to be heard, face to been seen, and anger and frustration to be acknowledged.

In conclusion, the words of Topsy, who seeks to dismantle evil, are apt:

> being women all the time
> is like breathing in and out
> it is like finding yourself in the midst of degradation
> and having the will to stake a claim for liberation
> it is like turning and turning and turning into a shimmering tomorrow
> it is like hearing a still, small voice
> that you craft into a roaring wind
> as you see and feel wholeness as no longer an abstract, sterile category
> but what we all yearn for
> so black women can, if we must, begin with the wounds
> those scars, in Eula's word, that are our mothers', daughters', sisters'
> the folds of those old wounds, that in some cases maimed us
> with lies, secrets, and silences we are told about other women
> that are told about ourselves
> these wounds mark us, but they do not need to define us.[12]

Theological Themes

> Black women's narratives counter . . . [the] assumptions and stereotypes embrace and discern a religious standard that exposes the moral hypocrisy of the planter class . . . [black] women are living witnesses to the power of divine grace . . . [enabling] them to turn victimization into . . . triumph.
>
> —Harriet Jacobs, *Incidents in the Life of a Slave Girl*

> Beloved, do not be surprised at the fiery ordeal that is taking place among you to test you, as though something strange were happening to you. But rejoice insofar as you are sharing Christ's sufferings, so that you may also be glad and shout for joy when his glory is revealed.
>
> —1 Peter 4:12–13

---

12. Townes, *Womanist Ethics*, 145.

> But as servants of God we have commended ourselves in every way: through great endurance, in afflictions, hardships, calamities, beatings, imprisonments, riots, labors, sleepless nights, hunger.
>
> —2 Corinthians 6:4–5

The theological themes that arose out of the therapy group were suffering and endurance, love and grace. As each woman shared her narrative, those themes were present. The theme of suffering and endurance can be seen in how the group participants coped with their experiences of oppression and violence, which suggests the presence of evil. Each participant used her faith, education—or both—to cope with her experiences of oppression and violence. This section explores suffering and endurance, and love and quiet grace. The themes of sin and evil will be explored in the final theological discussion and discourse section of this paper.

To gain insight into suffering and endurance as it relates to the African American women participants, I will illustrate meaning through the use of African American poetry and Negro spirituals. African American poet Carolyn Rodgers used her pen to give voice and raise consciousness to the black experience. Her words paint pictures that embody the generational impact of the suffering and endurance of black women from their experience of slavery, sexual violence, and oppression, and later focus on transformation, hope, and religion.

In her poem, *How I Got Ovah*, Rodgers writes:

> i can tell you...
> have swam for strength...
> and kissed my ancestors of the dirt
> whose rich dark root fingers rose up reached out...
> carried me...
> crossed rivers
> though I shivered...
> and wanted to sink down...[13]

In this particular poem, Rodgers illustrates suffering and endurance as she describes the depth of her tears, her strength, and the strength and support of her ancestors. Reading the poem one can feel the emotional fortitude which undergirds the need to endure. But the poem also suggests that

---

13. Rodgers, "How I Got Ovah," 759.

PSYCHOLOGICAL, SOCIOCULTURAL, AND THEOLOGICAL THEMES

suffering and endurance are part of her plight as a black woman. Moreover, it contends that endurance is predicated upon those who have gone before her, allowing her to draw from their strength. This has been asserted by Tanya who states, "I cried and I cried until I felt like I was dehydrated, but then I prayed and told God, 'Thank you for the strength, allowing me to make it through another.'" And by Abbie, who shared, "I cried ... anything could set me off ... dealing with the rejection of my husband and subsequent divorce. ... But I thank God for the strength." Dianne confirms the assertion, claiming, "I trust God and I have to cry out to God in prayer. When I can't, the stressors of life or my past experiences or situation weigh on me."

A similar assertion can be said drawing upon the spiritual *Guide Me, O Thou Great Jehovah*, composed by Welshman Williams (1717–1791) and translated into English by Peter Williams (1772–1796):

> Guide me, O Thou great Jehovah,
> Pilgrim through this barren land;
> I am weak, but Thou art mighty,
> Hold me with Thy pow'rful hand ...
> Let the fire and cloudy pillar,
> Lead me all my journey through,
> Strong Deliv'rer, strong Deliv'rer,
> Be Thou still my Strength and Shield ...
> Lord, I trust Thy mighty power,
> Wondrous are Thy works of old,
> Thou deliver'st Thine from thralldom,
> Who for naught themselves had sold,
> Thou didst conquer, Thou didst conquer[14]

This is one of many hymns that provides an account of the strength and endurance in the black church which depicts not only endurance but trust in God for deliverance. Moreover, it suggests two things about the experiences that are faced on the journey: (1) that they are not alone, and (2) that God is able to provide them strength and support. Olivia shares, "I thank God for strength I was able to endure the abuse of my husband and his mother, and when God made a way for me to leave I left. I'm grateful he was there to carry me through." Karen's words echo those of Olivia: "I am grateful to God—I am a woman who was abandoned as a child ...

---

14. Carpenter et al., *African Hymnal*, 693.

father died when I was eleven months old. I grew up with deficits, but God brought me through and that's why I trust him." The suffering and endurance highlighted in the narratives of the women demonstrate their trust and faith in God, that God is their source of strength. Their words illustrate a relational God who is "making a way out of a no way" and helping them to survive and triumph over their experience.[15]

Listening can be seen as a theme of love and quiet grace. Love demonstrated by the listener(s) is grace given to the narrator, as well as grace the storyteller gives to herself as each has a desire to explore the truth and to acknowledge her-story. The listener's feelings and thoughts undergird the narrative of each group participant and their ability to hold her-story. Love and grace will now be explored through a womanist lens, engaging the voices of Cheryl Townsend, Diana Hayes, Katie Cannon, Mae Henderson, and Zora Neale Hurston.

Beginning with the "loves" explored by Alice Walker, Townsend asserts that love of "the folk," love of "struggle," and love of oneself, "regardless," lays the foundation of a womanist love ethic, whereby Walker creates a context to re-humanize the experience of the black woman—creating a space for black women to create a "beloved community" that affirms their experience and one another on their journey towards survival and wholeness.[16] Hayes states, "Love heals inner wounds, stops pity parties, and aids black women and men to non-violently confront oppression and to persist regardless."[17] Listening allowed this author, as well as the group participants, to demonstrate a love for one another through our listening and space-making to heal the inner wounds of those sharing. Additionally, listening created a "beloved community" that allowed those present to demonstrate love for each woman, regardless of her experience, making it possible for the narrator to see herself and her story in a re-humanization context—positioning her to confront her oppression and/or experience of violence within a "beloved community" that was willing to journey with her through the sharing of her story of survival and hopes of wholeness and healing.

Cannon explores quiet grace and examines the underlying works of Hurston as a "search for truth."[18] Cannon asserts that "Hurston's charac-

15. Kirk-Duggan, *Misbegotten Anguish*, 12.
16. Townsend, "Loves Troubles," 89.
17. Crawford, *Hope in the Holler*, 99.
18. Cannon, *Womanist Ethics*, 125–28.

ters look at the world with their own eyes, form their own judgments, and demythologize whole bodies of so-called legitimacy. Encouraged by the oral-aural wisdom of the community, these women and men consider the inferences and recover the deeper meaning of life by reflecting on their own experiences."[19]

Henderson gives her interpretation of Hurston's *Their Eyes Were Watching God*.[20] She highlights the role of Pheoby Watson as listener who gives testimony to Janie Crawford's story. Henderson describes Pheoby's role as "earwitness" [listener], which emphasizes the importance and power of listening and its ability to be transformative.[21] The role of the listener demonstrates one's willingness and ability to open up one's self to hear the narrative and create space for the storyteller to give her testimony of her life—her struggles and life experiences.[22] This not only empowers the teller, but also listener, demonstrating both love and grace, in addition to empowerment. For this author, one's ability to listen demonstrates a theology of love and grace that allows the storyteller to affirm her story, as well as that of the listener.

To summarize, the therapy sessions and reflective journaling of the women participants demonstrated that, for black women, spirituality and their relationship with God is important and offers them a source of security, allowing them to exist in the midst of their harmful and injurious life experiences. This is evidenced by the statements shared by the participants:

> *Diane*: God is my source of strength and helps me to cope with multiple sclerosis.
>
> *Abbie*: Even in my struggle I trust God, and when I left nursing to go into ministry, he continues to provide the things I need. (Breaks down) I just pray, as I pull back and not deal with my pain—I'm learning to be transparent before God and asking how to be more for Abbie, as I seek God more daily, and deal with my loneliness, rejection, and pain.
>
> *Tanya*: Although my world seemed upside down, God has been my source of strength, even in my most difficult times.

---

19. Cannon, *Womanist Ethics*, 127.
20. Henderson, *Speaking Tongues*.
21. Henderson, *Speaking Tongues*, 11–12.
22. Henderson, *Speaking Tongues*, 11–12.

> *Erica*: I'm grateful to be here and all that God has brought me through.

Their spirituality and relationship with God, as depicted by their words, concerns a relational God, one who is able to be present even in the face of obstacles, difficulty, and despair. The women in this study have always been able to rely on God, and God has been a source of strength. Each woman explained how praying in moments of despair has been their greatest source of comfort and strength.

Jacqueline Mattis explores prayer as a source of strength for black women. She writes, "African American women, as they deal with race, class, and gender oppression . . . use prayer to cope with multiple levels of hardship."[23] That said, the awareness of the pastoral counselor using empathic listening will aide in understanding and creating space for black women to allow their whole self to be present in the therapeutic encounter. This allows black women to deconstruct negative theology, as well as negative life experiences, re-define what it means to be a strong black woman as they explore endurance and suffering, learn other healthy ways to cope, in addition to their spirituality, and move from being a fractured self to a whole self that embraces their humanity.

Theological Reflection and Discussion of Discourse

> So God created humankind in [God's] image, in the image of God—[God] created them; male and female.
>
> —Genesis 1:27

> God said to Moses, "I AM WHO I AM." This is what you are to say to the Israelites: "I AM has sent me to you." God also said to Moses, "Say to the Israelites, 'The LORD, the God of your fathers—the God of Abraham, the God of Isaac, and the God of Jacob—has sent me to you.' This is my name forever, the name by which I am to be remembered from generation to generation."
>
> —Exodus 3:14–15

---

23. Mattis, "Jesus is Your Savior," 148.

Death and life are in the power of the tongue.

—Proverbs 18:21

I prophesied as I had been commanded; and as I prophesied, suddenly there was a noise, a rattling, and the bones came together, bone to its bone. I looked, and there were sinews on them, and flesh had come upon them, and skin had covered them; but there was no breath in them. Then he said to me, "Prophesy to the breath, prophesy, mortal, and say to the breath: Thus says the Lord God: Come from the four winds, O breath, and breathe upon these slain, that they may live." I prophesied as he commanded me, and the breath came into them, and they lived, and stood on their feet, a vast multitude.

—Ezekiel 37:7–10

To conclude the exploration of theological themes, I will explore the matter of evil and several theologians' perspectives on evil. As I examine the evil and sin inflicted upon African American women, people created in the image of God, by persons who are also created in the image of God, I wrestle with that tension using my own voice. This discourse has been part of this author's journey and her re-construction of her theology.

The theological implications of the stories of the African American women participants in this study and the research data interwoven presented themes of sin and evil, salvation and redemption. Sin and evil was perpetrated on the mental and emotional being of those black women, creating a discourse of inner tension and conflict, fracturing their identity as evil and sin was interjected into their narratives, histories presented in this book. These women were not treated as a neighbor as Jesus instructs in Matthew's gospel. The kindness, love, and compassion one would provide themselves, or the reverence and love one might accord God was also absent in the lives of these women. That caused harm to their minds, bodies, and souls.

My understanding of evil is the absence of good love, and/or compassion. J. Nkansah-Obrempong describes evil as "any act, object, or behavior that threatens a person's relationship with God, as well as his or her well-being or that of fellow human beings."[24] My understanding of sin is

24. Dyrness et al., *Global Dictionary*, 300.

to miss the mark. Those who oppress, violate, deny, devalue, dehumanize, and hinder persons from seeing themselves in the image of God miss the mark. Williams understands sin as "participation in the large social systems that devalue black women's humanity through a process of devaluation and invisibilization."[25]

The formation of my theology is rooted in Matthew 22:36–40:

> Teacher, which commandment in the law is the greatest? He said to him, "You shall love the Lord your God with all your heart, and with all your soul, and with all your mind." This is the greatest and first commandment. And a second is like it: "You shall love your neighbor as yourself." On these two commandments hang all the law and the prophets.

This particular pericope informs my theology and is the starting point for approaching evil and sin. The scripture passage demonstrates (1) we must love God with our entire being, (2) we are mandated to love, (3) inner love is necessary—in order to love others we must be able to love ourselves, and (4) the value of relationship/community. This reasoning also raises the question: What is/was the condition of the self of those who perpetrated oppression and violence against black women? Finally, this viewpoint creates space to explore the emotional and mental framework of those who oppress and violate others, and their rejection of the instructions provided in Matthew 22:36–40. This leads to the posit that those who oppressed and violated projected hate—and that behavior calls into question their relationship with God and denies community.

Feminist therapist Maria Root uses the term "insidious trauma" to suggest that trauma is associated with oppression and the denial of the communal experience that is predicated upon ones racial, sexual, or class identification.[26] Further, Kyeong Hwangbo follows the conjecture of "insidious trauma," stating that "racism has the power to instigate intergenerationally transmitted trauma, in its relationships with other social factors such as gender, class, and age, produces synergistic effects of multiple marginization."[27] Both Root and Hwangbo assert the harm that can be inflicted upon others when they are denied the communal experience due to forms of oppression. Lastly, theologian Dietrich Bonhoeffer believed in the importance of being in relationship with God and one another, and that the

25. Coleman, *Making Way Out*, 20.
26. Gillespie, *Toni Morrison*, 242.
27. Gillespie, *Toni Morrison*, 242.

breaking of the relationship or the inability to be in relationship is how we fall short of the glory of God and sin against God.[28]

My understanding of a theology of grace, as explored earlier, is illustrated by what Cannon describes as quiet grace. Quiet grace is the search for truth.[29] The women participants came to the study seeking a safe and sacred space to lament and share their narratives and explore their experiences of oppression and violence. In the group structure, grace was embodied through each woman as she shared her story and listened to the stories of the other group participants and was able to hold each woman's truth.

Theologian Howard Thurman asserts that the development of one's personality needs love in order for one to become a functional human being. Thurman believes that when love has not been present that there is a need for understanding and acceptance, which causes one to desire being cared for.[30] The women came into the group armored. However, the quiet grace and love that was experienced in the space allowed them to become unarmored and share their stories. Further, in the sharing of the stories relationships, a "beloved community" was established. Thurman contends that adults are seeking to be in relationships that are real. They desire to have an even exchange of expression of love and caring one to another. He notes, "There is no feeling quiet comparable to the adult feeling that someone cares for you as you, without any extras involved. Each person longs for the kind of relationship with others in which it is no longer necessary to pretend in any sense whatsoever."[31]

Tanya, in her journal writing, expressed her desire for romantic love. However, towards the end of the group's journey, she was able to voice the love she developed over the group process for the women who created space for her and her woundedness. She states, "Everybody is not worth my nakedness, but I'm grateful that I was able to be naked and real in this space. I love each of you and the experience that was created in this group." The theme of grace and love from the group process demonstrated mutuality among the women and the pastoral counselor, exemplifying what Thurman and others refer to as interdependence. It was the communal aspect of the group, as examined by Ali, that allowed for lamenting, unarmoring, nakedness, trust, understanding, and acceptance among the participants. This, then, allowed

28. Ford et al., *Christian Theology*, 49–51.
29. Cannon, *Womanist Ethics*, 135.
30. Thurman, *Creative Encounter*, 106.
31. Thurman, *Creative Encounter*, 106.

for the journey of transformation, healing, and wholeness to begin. The personal experiences of this researcher, in addition to the doctoral journey, clinical group process, and inward and outward reflection leads her to conclude with language and thoughts on the power of spoken words, and the actions of love, sin, and evil. Additionally, they emphasize the need to create spaces where black women are able to hear life spoken, speak life over themselves, and affirm that they are created in the image of God, deconstruct negative stereotypes, and do what I call "re-construction" of identity.

Growing up, I remember the saying "sticks and stones may break your bones, but words will never hurt you." What a misleading notion that suggests that physical things have power to hurt, but spoken words do not hold any influence over your life. As an adult, I have come to realize that words have tremendous power—the words spoken to us and the words we speak to ourselves and to others. The impact of words on the psychic structure of black women is complex due to the layers of injurious harm towards their being—mind, body, and soul. Such harm can be termed insidious trauma, defined by Root as "traumatogenic efforts of oppression that are not necessarily overly violent or threatening to bodily well-being at the given moment but that do violence to the soul and spirit."[32] Although words were spoken that were injurious and harmful and created a fragmented self in some of the women, the group process allowed words of affirmation to speak life, words of encouragement to give support, and the practice of empathy to create a space that examined and deconstructed negative identities spoken into the lives of the African American women group participants. Abbie shares, "I was in the fourth grade when my teacher, out the blue, said I wouldn't be anything." Olivia states, "I have been called out of my name by my ex-husband and his mother—all because I wanted to have a voice." Tanya tells of words hurting when she says, "I remember wanting to run home from school cause the kids called me names." Karen proclaims, "We can no longer allow people to define who we are . . . or call us what they want to call us. . . . It's time to take ownership of the mislabels and reject them . . . and only answer by what we want to be known by."

A womanist framework attempts to help black women see, affirm, hear, make space, and empower black women and their narrative. Womanist theology is a starting point that not only affirms the black woman and her experience, but also provides a means of empathy through listening and understanding through a broader lens that begins with their experience

---

32. Caruth, *Trauma*, 107.

and makes space for culture, religion, and all things that helped to develop the identity of the black woman. A womanist method of providing care for black women is more than an approach. It is an understanding of their multiple-reality experience, and what may be spoken and unspoken within the dynamics of identifying as a black woman from the past, present, and future. Although black women are more than their experiences, it is their experiences that shape their understanding of self.

7

Conclusions

This chapter offers the researcher's model of group therapy for African American women identified as midwifing, a summary and discussion of the group process, data analysis, and recommendations for further research.

Midwifing

> The process of re-memory is best done in community. We remember the past to better inform our present activities.... Womanist concepts of salvation acknowledge that wholeness and survival come by remembering the past and learning from it.
>
> —Monica E. Coleman, *Ain't I a Womanist, Too?*

The theoretical concepts explored within womanist, self, and African-centered psychologies create a framework and theory that I implement to develop my understanding of "midwifing" as a womanist pastoral counseling method. The role of pastoral counselor as midwife is to support, empower, and meet counselees where they are. This allows for the counselee to transition from a state of survivor mode to thriving mode, thereby facilitating the creation of a safe and sacred space that allows the counselee to get through challenging life experiences. This framework also speaks of the power of language to transform and create healing.

In some folklore writing the midwife is referred to as "conjurer" or "sistah conjurer." Sistah conjurer is a term that, rather than "dismissing the women as superstitious or incompetent, gives them historical and personal agency [and] conjurer is a magical means of transforming reality.... It is a healing event ... taking healing as a metaphor for spiritual power. Black women emphasize the restorative potential ... locating in language a new curative domain."[1] The power of the black woman as conjurer, healer, or midwife is her ability to understand the plurality of black women's lived reality, use of language, and culture in order to provide healing to their entire being.[2]

A recent study on the role of midwives illustrates how midwifes allow women to become empowered by meeting them where they are, which in turn allows them to "get through" the birthing process.[3] This perspective provides a construct to engage the pastoral counselor on the benefits of meeting the counselee where she is in order to facilitate empowerment, thus allowing the entire person to be present in the therapeutic encounter of good, bad, and uncomfortable issues that may need to be explored (i.e., racism, sexism, classism, and other forms of oppression) when working with black women. The midwifing perspective suggests that the pastoral counselor must be in a position to hold, care for, and handle the issues that are a part of the counselee's narrative. I have interpreted this statement as a metaphor for women trying to get through and overcome difficult and traumatizing life experiences.

The narrative and midwifery experience of Margaret Charles Smith highlights the struggles of black women whom she cared for, and her ability to hold all that their lived reality represented as she cared for them and created a space to prepare for the birthing. Linda Holmes writes "Mrs. Smith's skills as a midwife stood up to many of the challenges she faced, allowing her, as black folks often say, to 'make a way out of no way.' . . . Mrs. Smith met few problems that she couldn't solve."[4] Womanist and women's healthcare provider Arisika Razak explains her experience of a midwife as someone who "stand[s] as witness, companion, and helper. . . . My work [as a midwife] demonstrated the immense contradictions under which women live."[5] Razak goes on to share how her experience as a midwife created and encountered a holiness experience, whereby the face of God was able to be experienced in the birthing process.[6] The birth process in midwifing would be to journey alongside counselees as they are able to develop a functional process for externalizing—giving birth, if you will, to their hurt

1. Lee, *Granny Midwives*, 14–17.
2. Lee, *Granny Midwives*, 12–19.
3. Cooper et al., "Women's Perceptions Midwife's," 268.
4. Smith and Holmes, *Listen to Me Good*, 88.
5. Razak, "Embodying Womanism," 218.
6. Razak, "Embodying Womanism," 218.

and pain of oppressive and violent life experiences and encountering the face of God through the telling, thereby creating space for new life. A midwifing therapeutic approach is aware of the importance of creating a safe and sacred space that allows the pastoral counselor to build trust with the counselee in order to hear her story. Trust is important when working with African American women because of their unique experience of violence and/or oppression. Safety allows the counselee to trust and be open to exploring their feelings and thoughts.

Lee highlights the trust aspect midwifing throughout her book, *Granny, Midwives and Black Women Writers: Double-Dutched Readings*, as she explores the perception of midwives from those for whom she provides care. Asserting midwife Miss Mary, Lee writes, "When patients saw the midwife coming, they thought they saw heaven! They thought the midwife could ease their burdens for them."[7] This suggests not only the healing aspect of the perception of the midwife, but her connection to God and a feeling of safety and trust that engenders for women in her care. Engaging the voice of Holmes, who writes, "the ability to summon the Holy Ghost for support, guidance, and 'miracle working,' . . . midwives frequently assumed the meditative state of prayer in preparation of attending a birth,"[8] Lee explores the "high and holy calling" of granny midwives who note they received a "call from the Lord" to do midwifery, thereby relying upon the spiritual dimensions of God to use their gift of "catching the baby."[9]

For this researcher, "catching the baby" can be used as a metaphor for the pastoral counselor's ability to not only offer a container, but also to be able to hold the narratives of the black women as they fill the container.[10] It is the belief of this researcher that when the pastoral counselor establishes trust and safety, the counselee is more likely to permit their entire being into the counseling session and share their narrative. The pastoral counselor as midwife creates a therapeutic environment facilitating the counselee's becoming unarmored. Becoming unarmored is critical when working with black women as they have armored themselves in order to survive in a world where they have been subjected to racism, sexism, and classism. These forms of violence and oppression made it necessary for them to operate out of a survival mode. In order for African American women to tell their story and

---

7. Lee, *Granny Midwives*, 86.
8. Smith and Homes, *Listen to Me Good*, 88.
9. Lee, *Granny Midwives*, 82–83.
10. Lee, *Granny Midwives*, 84.

achieve healing, they must be afforded a safe and sacred space that honors their story and experience. Further, the pastoral counselor must have the fortitude to hold and engage their story.

In order for that safe and sacred space to occur, the pastoral counselor must develop a position of empathy. Empathy allows for the counselee to remain unarmored and open to engage their story with the pastoral counselor, and examine their defense mechanisms. Lee's use of the metaphor "double-dutched readings" illustrates empathy as she places herself, as well as, other folklore and literary writers, in the shoes of those who have provided care to black women. Their desire is to tell the stories not from their lens, but through the lens of the women who are sharing their stories and experiences. Lee and other writers, such as Morrison, do not change the narrative to fit the experiences of today, but hold the story in the light in which the giver shared their experiences—or "herstory." Lee illustrates empathy throughout her writing as she engages the narratives of the granny midwives and places herself in their shoes, as if it is her story. She carefully tells it so as not to assume it as her own, utilizing listening and understanding to craft the stories through the lenses of granny midwives.[11]

Thus, midwifing is an attempt at listening and understanding the stories and experiences of the black woman through their lenses. This creates an opportunity, in which the black woman can be heard, let down her defenses, and know that it is safe to tell her story. When black women are able to tell their story, it is an invitation for them to hear their story and reflect on their experience, and the reasons they have become armored. They can then inspect their defense mechanisms, allowing them to explore and get to the root of their armoring. When black women are met where they are, it invites them to risk being transparent and discard their mask of defenses. This positions them to gain insight into self and how armoring has played a role in their building relationships and identifying self. Exploring the "why" helps to externalize negative feelings and thoughts that may have prevented them from building a healthier self-image and relationships with others.

Midwifing, as a womanist approach to pastoral counseling, creates an opportunity for affirmation and understanding as the counselee become unarmored and engage their story. Smith and Holmes state, "You are sitting there to do what you can for her, . . . rest her back . . . talk to her . . . talking kind words, giving kind words. . . . Kindness whipped the evil."[12] The telling

---

11. Lee, *Granny Midwives*, 103.
12. Smith and Holmes, *Listen to Me Good*, 89.

of their story authorizes counselees to honor their voice, story, and identity, thus allowing them to become empowered. Through listening and affirming, pastoral counselors have the ability to journey with the counselee to un-armor and re-story a new beginning, allowing them to not only uncover painful memories, but to move past them—not allowing their past to define them.

This counseling method not only helps the counselee to become empowered, it also provides a space for them to recognize their humanity. When this occurs, she is able to become empowered and liberated from negative experiences. As a result, the counselee is able to deconstruct negative experiences, stereotypes, forms of oppression, and other experiences that contributed to the fragmented self, allowing for the development of a healthy core self and relationships within their community, and to see themselves in the image of God. Using birthing as a metaphor, black women can let go of their pain. Exploring the pain is an attempt to get the counselee to acknowledge and voice their experiences of oppression and violence, and to lament—which will allow them to move towards thriving. Smith and Holmes state, "Well honey child, you are going to have to hurt before your baby is born. It ain't no way around that. . . . I want you to be aware of what's coming . . . and do the best you can."[13] This statement demonstrates the importance of acknowledging the pain the counselee feels. It also asserts that in order to journey alongside the counselee as they explore their feelings, the pastoral counselor must be patient. Smith and Holmes note, "You've got to be patient to be a midwife. . . . Talk consolation. . . . Some people have hard long labor"[14] Recognizing the relevance of empathy and listening to understand denotes the patience pastoral counselors must have in order to engage the complex narratives of black women seeking healing. Empathy, listening, and patience are essential in creating opportunities for black women to move past merely surviving to thriving and becoming a cohesive self.

In conclusion, affirming, healing, restoring, empowering, and liberating in the therapeutic encounter allows and creates a safe and sacred space for black women to see themselves in the image of God. It allows them to see a God who is on the side of the oppressed, encouraging them to free themselves from oppressive forces and journey with God who created them in God's likeness. This enables them to learn and demonstrate self-love and deconstruct self-hate. Thus, Black women can accept and receive care from

---

13. Smith and Holmes, *Listen to Me Good*, 90.
14. Smith and Holmes, *Listen to Me Good*, 90.

the pastoral care provider who invites them to become empowered and re-position themselves from a place of invisibility to visibility through the works of healing, sustaining, guiding, nurturing, empowering, liberating, and reconciling, allowing them to embrace their humanity. This moves them from a fractured state to cohesive state where they are able to achieve external and internal wholeness in self-exploration and understanding of self, God, and community.

Summary and Discussion of the Group

In this section I discuss the clinical group process, group participants, their journals, and the researcher's log, emphasizing the "why" behind the armoring, isolation, and diminished identity of African American women who have experienced various forms of oppression and violence. Additionally, the discussion illustrates the resiliency of African American women as they accept, embrace, own, and determine who they are through their own lenses, and move toward their re-storying.

In chapter three I outlined the theoretical framework, using a womanist theology integrated with self-psychology and African-centered psychology to create a midwifing approach for providing pastoral care and counseling for African American women who have experienced various forms of oppression and violence in the United States. The womanist imagery of midwifing is used to symbolize the power of support, safety, mutuality, and understanding in relationship with women to help sustain women giving birth. From this researcher's lens, the pain experienced in birth is manageable because of the support of the midwife and her assistants who meet the mothers' needs as she desires to release the baby she has been carrying for nine months. For this researcher, this suggests that African American women have been carrying the burdens placed on them by society and their past, hindering them from fully living. Rather, they have simply existed because they have not been able to release the harmful and injurious experiences of the past—their past and the past of their ancestors. The injurious past includes memories of slavery, segregation, dehumanization, rape, beatings, lynching, negative and false identities projected on them by others, rejection by their mothers, fathers, families, internal and external communities, and by Western society.

Several women participating in this study shared that they are exploring other denominations and avenues of providing ministry and serving

God, and have their church because of various forms of oppression during the course of their ministry there. Further, each participant shared that their experience of oppression and violence has not affected their relationship with God. This study also revealed that a form of coping for the women was education. Several women had two master's degrees and were working toward a third. One participant was in her second year of her doctoral program, while another had obtained her doctorate, and another was applying to a doctoral program. Each woman expressed how education played a major role in allowing her to cope with the experiences of abandonment, molestation, rape, and rejection.

Many of the women in this study explored their feelings of inadequacy, shame, worthlessness, guilt, and depression. Four of the six women stated that their feelings created a diminished self-esteem and identity, causing them to isolate themselves when not working in the church and ministry. Additionally, each explored their inability to develop and/or maintain healthy male-coupled, loving relationships, and three of the women have settled into singlehood as a result of the difficulty of forming healthy male-coupled relationships. Further, they reported that they try to keep busy in order not to deal with injurious and harmful past experiences. It was easier to keep busy than work through the pain. Busyness allowed them to exist and function.

Data Analysis

The group case study demonstrated the remnants of slavery and the impact it continues to have on the psyche of black women and their identity, ability to trust, and to build relationships with black men and women. After reviewing the group sessions, journals, and researcher's logs, the data also demonstrate the impact of violence and oppression on black women by other black women. Additionally, throughout the sessions, the women used the terms fragmented and fragmentation to explain how they identified themselves as a result of their experience and socialization, and their desire to be free and whole.

Throughout the group sessions the women shared their excitement that a study was being done to explore the need for adequate and safe space where they can take off their masks and reveal themselves to someone would be able to handle what they had to share. Additionally, they indicated that they internalize their feelings because they do not want to burden anyone with their concerns, hurts, and pain. Moreover, the group case study revealed the need to explore the racism experienced between black women. That topic was not explored in-depth by this researcher. Further research is needed to the impact of racism among black women on the fragmentation of black women and the decline of healthy the relationship among black women.

Each participant affirmed that they are women of African American descendant and students attending the Interdenominational Theological Center in Atlanta, Georgia. All of the women confirmed that they have experienced some form of violence and/or oppression. Each participated shared that she had no prior relationship or knowledge of this researcher or the clinical supervisor for this research project. All the women participating in the study stated that they have experienced forms of racism, sexism, or classism. Each woman answered "yes" to the question "Have you experienced sexual, physical, or emotional abuse?" Five women answered "no" and one answered "yes" to the question "Do you ever struggle with your identity as a black woman?" All answered "yes" to the question "Do you consider yourself a strong black woman?" One woman answered "yes" and five answered "no" to the question "Do you believe there are other ethnicities more superior to you as an African American woman?" To the question "Do you know who you are as a black woman?" one group participant answered "no," one choose not to answer and stated, "I am a Christian woman and I don't know how to respond to this answer," and four women answered "yes." The final question, "Do you feel like you have had adequate space to grieve or lament the negative experiences in your life?" four women answered "yes" and two answered "no."

Out of the six group participants, only one woman was aware of which generation since the emancipation of enslaved Africans she is a part. She had this knowledge as a result of being raised in a home where there was a strong African presence both in historical knowledge and education, and in identifying as African descendant. Two other women participants were raised in a Christian home. One of those women was taught not to see color, while the other was made aware of color and her "black" features. Race, ethnicity, history, and culture were not spoken of or taught in her home. Another group participant was raised in a military family by her biological mother and step-father. She had no relationship with her biological father who is now deceased. Her family lived in a predominately white neighborhood where race, ethnicity, history, and culture were not discussed. A fifth participant was raised by her maternal aunt and uncle, to whom she refers as her parents. (Her biological mother and father were in their early teens when she was born and currently live in another state raising their other children). Although race, ethnicity, history, and culture were not taught in the home, she learned of her identity in the school systems through black activists. Finally, the sixth group participant was raised by her mother and recalled being treated unfairly by her family because of her "black" features and skin tone. She has no knowledge of family history. And since race, ethnicity, history, and culture were not taught in her home, within her family and community "black" was bad.

The other questions explored in group will be examined in the categories of identity, oppression and violence, and stereotypes. The clinical group case study illustrates that women of African descent continue to deal with various forms of oppression and violence. They each described a wide array of feelings that include sadness, depression, anger, shame, numbness, stress, negative thoughts, emptiness, loneliness, rejection, grief, and anxiety. Functioning as learner, I utilized ethnographic listening to suspend judgment, seek understanding, gain clarity, and created a space that allowed the participants' story to be magnified and made larger.[15] This allowed this researcher to establish an atmosphere that allowed participants to engage their feelings, deconstruct the negative identification of their past, and re-story their present. Each participant was able to explore and discover the root of emotions that began in childhood and continue today in adulthood.

For some of the women, this was their first time to publicly lament and grieve. They openly shared for the first time their experiences of sexual trauma, from gang rape to familial rape. Some spoke of physical and emotional abuse by spouse and family members, and oppression experienced in corporate America, religious denominations, and in relationships with a spouse or significant other. Out of the six participants, four women experienced sexual abuse, and each experienced several forms of emotional and physical abuse in the context of internal and external family relationships. Their narratives speak to the fragmentation of self, as highlighted throughout my research.

The research also shows a correlation between black women's identity and their experience of oppression and violence. Of the six group members, one was gang raped and molested, another was molested by a family member, and two were raped and molested by family members. Of those

---

15. Moschella, *Ethnography*, 143.

participants raised in a two-parent home, four of the parents are still married. The parents of the participant raised in a two-parent home by her maternal aunt and uncle and those of the participant raised by her mother and step-father are now divorced.

The research reveals the importance of coping resources for black women other than their spirituality. Black women must have a place of safety where they can lament and work through their internal conflicts and life stressors. Counseling and spirituality for African American women are able to work together to help them explore and manage their feelings associated with oppression and violence. Thus, it was important for this researcher to create a safe and sacred space, and develop trust with each woman in the group so that each group participant could begin to explore the painful past that continues to enslave her.

The research group met in the Thomas J. Pugh Counseling Center, located on the campus of Interdenominational Theological Center, an historical Black seminary located in an historic district of Atlanta, where African American civil rights leaders and other community leaders were once prominent. The area is now in decline and an impoverished neighborhood. The location and environment of the group meeting helped to facilitate healing. It allowed for the ancestors to be present as the group reflected on the lives of their ancestors and their pain, hurt, and grief they expressed through embodiment, as well as voice. Reflecting on the impact of African American ancestors, civil rights leaders, and the safety represented by the Thomas J. Pugh Counseling Center, named for the father of pastoral counseling for African Americans and located on the campus where Howard Thurman and others once walked, created a unique healing experience that each participant and this researcher was able to explore within the research sessions.

The group case study was important for the researcher because it created an opportunity for black women to share, listen, hear, learn, and support each other. Creating a safe and sacred space that allowed each participant to feel safe, as well as become unarmored, was essential in order to develop trust with the pastoral counselor and other group participants. Additionally, affording the women a space to externalize painful experiences, harmful identities, and internalize a new story created and fostered wholeness, healing, and transformation among the group participants. Further, it provided an opportunity for this researcher to examine racism, classism, and sexism as forms of violence in the lives of black women and the impact of that violence on the identities of the women, while creating an environment that allowed for healing to occur in a communal and supportive space among other black women.

At the good-bye session, each participant received a note card that read, "I just gotta be who I was made to be . . . Me. 'I will praise thee; for I am fearfully and wonderfully made' (Psalm 139:14)." We discussed how they were able to view themselves at the close of the group compared to how they viewed themselves at the beginning of the group. The group permitted the women a space to share, hear, and listen to their experiences and the experiences of each woman from their context. This communal response allowed for vulnerability and set an atmosphere in which the women could lament. As pastoral counselor, the group afforded me the opportunity to mirror, at least some of the time, a healthy culture that affirmed their experience, dismantled some negative stereotypes, and allowed us to explore themes of rejection projected onto me in their transference, as well as, bracket my countertransference of rejection. The benefits of the group allowed each woman to engage their psychological developmental and the impact of cultural on their self-images. At times the dialogue within the group was experienced as intense and energetic, demonstrating that no subject was off limits and that a safe container was available for holding any feelings and statements. This allowed for the real relationship to be demonstrated in the therapeutic encounter between the pastoral counselor and the group participants thus portraying an image of midwifing. The genuine connection within the group allowed for conflicts to be explored, inner shame to be deconstructed, negative stereotypes to be re-framed, faith and spirituality to be examined, and other ways of coping to be explored.

Recommendations for Further Research

The most significant limitation of this study is its inability to capture the voices of African American women on a larger scale, and its lack of focus on violence and oppression experienced by other African American women. Because of time and other constraints, the study could give voice to only a small number of African American women living in the metropolitan Atlanta area, in a narrow age-range, and all of whom share the experience of attending a historically black college or university. This small population does not speak to the experiences of black women throughout the United States or of other lands where African descendants were dropped as a result of slavery. Further research on a larger scale is necessary to gain a broader understanding of African American women's experience. That research should include a survey of poor, uneducated, and disadvantaged black women.

Appendix A

IBR Protocol Proposal

What are your key research questions?

a. The main research question for this study is: How can group therapy help African American women heal from a fractured sense of self based on violence and oppression?

b. Sub-questions that are also essential to the study are: How do (some?) Black women become fragmented? How does this fragmentation hinder them in the world and impact their ability to build healthy relationships and a healthy self-identity? Lastly, what external factors in their lived reality foster this fragmented (identification of) self?

What are the objectives and purposes of this research?

The objectives and purposes of this research are to:

a. Explore the condition and state of the identity of some Black women who have experienced any form of violence and oppression.

b. To demonstrate the need for culturally competent therapists to be equipped to work with some Black women who have experienced violence and oppression, resulting in a loss of self.

c. To demonstrate how listening and understanding creates a safe space for the participants to become unarmored, and mirrors new ways of healing and dealing with negative narratives.

What research methods do you plan to use?

This research project implements a Womanist theology and methodological lens used to examine the experiences of Black women and a case study method utilizing group therapy consisting of 6 African American female students over the age of 40 who have experienced violence and oppression. The group will meet 2 hours bi-weekly for 12 sessions.

How do you plan to begin your research?

a. Research will begin with an approved advertisement at The Interdenominational Theological Center (ITC). Followed by (1) an initial introduction of the research, (2) screening questions, (3) follow-up interview, and (4) prescreening questions and tool. All participants will not have any prior relationship with the researcher or the licensed professional counselor supervising the clinical research data. All interviews, prescreening tools and assessments, and counseling will be conducted at the Thomas J. Pugh Counseling Center on the campus of ITC.

b. This process will be supervised by a licensed professional therapist to ensure the care of the group participants and the researcher.

c. All women

Whose consent will you need to obtain? What documents will you use to explain your work? (Consent Forms follow Pre-Screening Questions)

Participants will be age 40 or above, who have demonstrated in the prescreening process that they are emotionally stable to participate in the group process. The consent form will include the following: (1) provide a clear description of the research project and potential risks and benefits of participation; (2) description of the questions to be explored; (3) ensure that the human subject has the right to answer or not to answer any question and that the answer given will be sufficient; (4) confidentiality agreement including the right to withdraw from the participation at any time; and (5) publication of research data in the dissertation upon completion as relates the participant.

What is your relationship to the people who will be part of the project?

There will be no prior relationship to the participants. During the group process my relationship will be as researcher, participant-observer, and pastor counselor.

What recruitment procedures do you plan to use?

APPENDIX A: IBR PROTOCOL PROPOSAL

I will use an approved advertising flyer to distribute, place, and display on campus of the ITC. (See Flyer, which follows Consent Form.)

What questions do you plan to ask? If you are using a questionnaire, please include a copy of it.

The research project will explore the following questions:

1. Are you an African American woman student at ITC?
2. Have you ever experienced some form of violence and/or oppression?
3. Do you have any prior relationship to Rev. Malone or Rev. Glenn?
4. Have you experienced any form of racism, sexism, or classism?
5. Have you experienced sexual, physical, or emotional abuse?
6. Do you ever struggle with your identity as a Black woman?
7. Do you consider yourself a strong Black woman?
8. Do you ever believe there are other ethnicities more superior to you as an African American woman?
9. Do you know who you are as a Black woman?
10. How much would you say you have been able to grieve or lament the negative experiences in your life?
11. What generation (since the Emancipation Proclamation of enslaved Africans) are you in your family?
12. Were you raised by one or both of your parents?
13. Do you like yourself?
14. Have you ever been sexually abused or exploited?
15. Please define how you see or identify yourself?
16. Describe any negative images of yourself and where they came from?
17. When was the first time you were sexually exploited or taken advantage of?
18. Were you ever raped or molested?
19. Do you ever have low self-esteem?
20. (If yes to #4): How many abusive relationships have you been in?

21. Describe your feelings after your experience of racism, sexism or classism?
22. (If you identify with the Strong Black Woman image, do you feel you are always strong/always have to be strong?
23. How and when might you be able to grieve or lament?

At the termination session, I will ask, "Reflecting on the group process can you share what you learned, what will you take with you, and what would you have liked to discuss and/or changed?" My final question will be, "In a sentence or using one word answer the question 'Who am I?'"

Group questioned throughout the group process will include:

The questions explored in the group process will be opened ended around the Black women's experience of oppression and violence to include but not limited to racism, sexism, classism, their relationship to God, faith, spirituality, worship, and/or the Black church, lamenting, and journaling process.

What are the potential benefits for persons who are part of the project?

The potential benefits are twofold: (1) It will benefit pastoral counselors who work with African American women by providing another lens or awareness to hear the true experience of some Black women who have experienced violence, and see past their armoring; (2) For Black women it will help them to deconstruct negative narratives, become unarmored, lament, and thrive.

What are potential risks for persons who are part of the project, including physical, mental, or social discomfort, harm, or danger?

Potential risk will be in the telling of their stories. If participants for any reason is unable to complete the group due to her inability to cope and/or manage self-care, the researcher will support and care for the participant toward accessing care and referring her for follow-up care with the staff counselor of the Thomas J. Pugh Counseling Center of the ITC.

How will you respond if any participant has adverse effects as a result of your research?

APPENDIX A: IBR PROTOCOL PROPOSAL

To prepare I will make myself available to provide additional brief pastoral care and support as needed during the project. To conclude the group process the final group session will be a wrap-up evaluation and "good bye" session to terminate our relationship, and provide referrals if needed, by pre-arrangement with the Thomas Pugh Center at ITC for free counseling, at the conclusion of the project.

The group therapy process will be supervised by a licensed professional counselor.

Will the project involve any deception of participants? If so, how? What procedures will you use to debrief participants?

The project will not involve any deception of the participants.

What alternative procedures are available to a subject who wishes to withdraw or who is damaged by the project?

The participants may withdraw at any time and I will provide them with referrals for other pastoral counselors if needed, as well as the staff counselor of the Thomas J. Pugh Counseling Center of the ITC.

How do you plan to protect the data? How will you protect confidentiality of the data?

All data will be password protected and secured in a locked filing system.

How and where will the research be reported/disseminated?

All research will be transcribed by the researcher and processed using qualitative software for data analysis. All data will be password protected and secured in a locked filing system. The research data will be reported in the dissertation, "Midwifing: A Womanist Approach to Pastoral Counseling Investigating the Fractured Self, Slavery, Violence, and the Black Woman." It is also probable that the dissertation may be reworked for standard practices and mainstream publication at a later date.

Appendix B

Prescreening Questions

1. Are you an African American woman student at ITC?
2. Have you ever experienced some form of violence and/or oppression?
3. Do you have any prior relationship to Rev. Malone or Rev. Glenn?
4. Have you experienced any form of racism, sexism, or classism?
5. Have you experienced sexual, physical, or emotional abuse?
6. Do you ever struggle with your identity as a Black woman?
7. Do you consider yourself a strong Black woman?
8. Do you ever believe there are other ethnicities more superior to you as an African American woman?
9. Do you know who you are as a Black woman?
10. How much would you say you have been able to grieve or lament the negative experiences in your life?

Appendix C

Consent Form

I, _____ hereby agree to participate in the above named research project and, if interviewed, to have my interview recorded and transcribed. I understand that my interview may be quoted in any final reporting of the project in print or online.

I do _____ do not_____ give permission to be quoted by name. I understand that I have the right not to answer any question /that any answer is acceptable; and I may stop my participation at any time, and that I may withdraw any or all of these consents at any time up to the final publication of project results by contacting the project director *in writing* at the email or street address listed above. If I have any questions about the project, I may write, email or phone the project director, clinical supervisor, or Chairperson of the Columbia Institutional Review Board at any time.

I do ____ do not____ give permission to be contacted with any follow-up questions following my survey/interview at The Interdenominational Theological Center

(if yes, please enter phone number or email address:)

_____

I would ____ would not _____ like to receive a summary of the final report. (if yes, please enter email or U.S. mailing address:)

_____

Signed (participant*): _____

Date _____

Signed (interviewer): _____

Date _____

Form updated 2-6-2012

APPENDIX C: CONSENT FORM

Consent Form, Continued

This project is being conducted in partial fulfillment of the Doctor of Theology degree at Columbia Theological Seminary.

The purpose of the project is to pilot test a group therapy method to address healing and transformation for *Black women who have experienced violence and/or oppression.*

The types of issues and questions you will be asked to respond to include:

Issues to be explored:

Black women's unique experiences of racism, sexism, and classism as forms of violence.

Screening Questions:

1. Are you an African American woman student at ITC?
2. Have you ever experienced some form of violence and/or oppression?
3. Do you have any prior relationship to Rev. Malone or Rev. Glenn?
4. Have you experienced any form of racism, sexism, or classism?
5. Have you experienced sexual, physical, or emotional abuse?
6. Do you ever struggle with your identity as a Black woman?
7. Do you consider yourself a strong Black woman?
8. Do you ever believe there are other ethnicities more superior to you as an African American woman?
9. Do you know who you are as a Black woman?
10. How much would you say you have been able to grieve or lament the negative experiences in your life?

Sample Questions and Issues to Be Explored in the Therapy Group (in addition to the screening questions above):

1. What generation (since the Emancipation Proclamation of enslaved Africans) are you in your family?
2. Were you raised by one or both of your parents?
3. Do you like yourself?
4. Have you ever been sexually abused or exploited?

APPENDIX C: CONSENT FORM

5. Please define how you see or identify yourself?
6. Describe any negative images of yourself and where they came from?
7. When was the first time you were sexually exploited or taken advantage of?
8. Were you ever raped or molested?
9. Do you ever have low self-esteem?
10. (If yes to #4): How many abusive relationships have you been in?
11. Describe your feelings after your experience of racism, sexism or classism?
12. (If you identify with the Strong Black Woman image): Do you feel you are always strong/always have to be strong?
13. How and when might you be able to grieve or lament?

Risks and Benefits: The potential risks and benefits of participation are: To minimize risk I will work with participants who are considered of legal age and who don't need the consent of a parent or legal guardian. To reduce potential risk of participants I will be available to provide additional pastoral care if needed throughout the project. Also, I will provide participants with referrals to seek counseling if they don't meet the research requirements. In conclusion the project will be supervised by a faculty member of the department of pastoral care at the Interdenominational Theological Center. The benefits of exploration may include the following, (1) allow Black women to hear their stories for the first time, (2) re-story their experience, and (3) deconstruct internal negative identifications of self-leading them to build and/or develop a healthy self.

The *Research Procedure* chosen for this project is:

- screening interviews
- reflective journaling
- clinical case study notes
- a research log
- group therapy meeting two hours for 12 sessions bi-weekly for 6 weeks

Confidentiality will be maintained by: *Myrna Thurmond-Malone*.

APPENDIX C: CONSENT FORM

Projected Outcomes: This project is intended to benefit pastoral counselors who provide care to African American women and African American women especially those who experienced forms of violence and oppression.

Costs and Payments: There are no costs for participation in this study. Participation is completely voluntary and no payments will be provided.

Contact and Questions: The researcher conducting this is: Rev. Myrna Thurmond-Malone. You may ask any questions you have now. If you have questions later, you are encouraged to contact her via email at revmyrnamalone@yahoo.com.

For further information, or if you have any questions, you may contact the faculty advisor, Dr. Pamela Cooper White, Cooperwhitep@ctsnet.edu.

You will be given a copy of this information to keep for your records.

Appendix D

Advertising Flyer

RESEARCH STUDY Midwifing: A Womanist Approach to Pastoral Counseling Investigating the Fractured Self, Slavery, Violence, and the Black Woman

Study Description: *This research study is designed to give voice to a model of therapy that promotes healing of the minds, bodies, and souls of women of African descent. Therefore the research study will explore a Womanist pastoral psychotherapeutic methodology that understands and is aware of the 'multiple-reality experience' of Black women, and their unique experiences of racism, sexism, and classism.*

FREE
Counseling Group for Women of African Descent

<u>Discussion Areas:</u>
Racism, Sexism, and Classism as forms of violence against Black women

Participation in this group is connected to a research study being conducted by Rev. Myrna Thurmond-Malone, a doctoral candidate at Columbia Theological Seminary. This research will explore the effects of violence and oppression against women of African descent.

This research group is designed to give voice to the unique experiences of women of African descent and their experiences of racism, sexism, and classism have been forms of violence and have shaped their theological and psychological structures.

Research Benefits:
The study results may be used to help counselors who plan to work with women of African descent women who have experienced forms of violence that include but are not limited to racism, sexism, and classism.

Study Participation Benefits:
- No-cost therapy group sessions and individual sessions if needed with a Pastoral Counselor

For more information, contact:

Clinical Investigator: Rev. Myrna Thurmond-Malone, M.Div., revmyrnamalone@yahoo.com, 404.907.0248

To participate in this study you must be:
- An African American woman student attending ITC.
- Experienced a form of violence and/or oppression.
- Complete an initial session with the Clinical Investigator to assess your readiness for the group.
- Be able to commit to 6 weeks of group sessions, bi-weekly for 2 hours.
- Are able to discuss your experiences in a group setting.
- Participant should not have any prior relationship to Rev. Myrna Thurmond-Malone or the clinical consultant, Dr. Ca Trice Glenn, LPC, NCC.

Exclusion criteria for this study:
- is based on the intake assessment
- participants must meet the above criteria

Appendix E

Prescreening Interview Assessment Tool

General Information:

Name: Last _____

       First _____ MI ____

Mailing Address: _____

                City: _____ State: _____

Leave a Yes ☐ No ☐

Phone: (____)_____

Email Address: _____

DOB: _____

Profession: _____

Religious Denomination/Spiritual Preference: _____
_____

     Have you ever participated in group counseling or received counseling previous in the past? _____. If so, when, how frequent, and type of therapy? _____
_____

APPENDIX E: PRESCREENING INTERVIEW ASSESSMENT TOOL

Racial/ethnic identity:

☐ African American/Black African ☐ Afro-Asian ☐ Siddi ☐ Africans in Guangzhou

☐ Indigenous/African Australians ☐ Balkans ☐ Afro-Europe ☐ Afro-Caribbean

☐ Other: _____

Marital Status:

☐ Single ☐ Engaged ☐ Married/Partnered ☐ Separated

☐ Divorced ☐ Widowed

Screening Interview Questions

Are you an African American/African descent woman student at ITC?	Yes ☐	No ☐
Have you ever experienced some form of violence and/or oppression?	Yes ☐	No ☐
Do you have any prior relationship to myself (Rev. Malone) or Rev. Glenn?	Yes ☐	No ☐
Have you experienced any form of racism, sexism, or classism?	Yes ☐	No ☐
Have you experienced sexual, physical, or emotional abuse?	Yes ☐	No ☐
Do you ever struggle with your identity as a Black woman?	Yes ☐	No ☐
Do you consider yourself a strong Black woman?	Yes ☐	No ☐
Do you ever believe there are other ethnicities more superior to you as an African American woman?	Yes ☐	No ☐
Do you know who you are as a Black woman?	Yes ☐	No ☐
Do you feel like you have had adequate spaces to grieve or lament the negative experiences in your life? _____	Yes ☐	No ☐

All Information is <u>CONFIDENTIAL</u>.

Office hours available Monday and Wednesday between the hours of 12:00 p.m. and 2:00 p.m. at the Thomas J. Pugh counseling center.

Appendix F

Prescreening Assessment Tool

Name: _____

Date: _____

    Below is a list of traumatic events or situations. Please mark YES if you have experienced or witnessed the following events or mark NO if you have not had that experience.

Serious accident, fire or explosion	Yes ☐	No ☐
Natural disaster (tornado, flood, hurricane, major earthquake)	Yes ☐	No ☐
Non-sexual assault by someone you know (physically attacked/injured)	Yes ☐	No ☐
Non-sexual assault by a stranger	Yes ☐	No ☐
Sexual assault by a family member or someone you know	Yes ☐	No ☐
Sexual assault by a stranger	Yes ☐	No ☐
Military combat or a war zone	Yes ☐	No ☐
Sexual contact before you were age 18 with someone who was 5 or more years older than you	Yes ☐	No ☐
Imprisonment	Yes ☐	No ☐
Torture	Yes ☐	No ☐
Life-threatening illness	Yes ☐	No ☐
Other traumatic event	Yes ☐	No ☐

If "other traumatic event" is checked YES above; please write what the event was
_____

Of the question to which you answered YES, which was the worst _____ (Please list the question #)

Which of the above incidences is the reason for which you are currently seeking treatment? (Please list the question #)

APPENDIX F: PRESCREENING ASSESSMENT TOOL

If you answered *NO* to all of the above questions, *STOP*.

If you answered *YES* to any of the above questions, please complete the rest of the form.

Please check YES or NO regarding the event listed in question 15.

Were you physically injured?	Yes ☐	No ☐
Was someone else physically injured?	Yes ☐	No ☐
Did you think your life was in danger?	Yes ☐	No ☐
Did you think someone else's life was in danger?	Yes ☐	No ☐
Did you feel helpless?	Yes ☐	No ☐
Did you feel terrified?	Yes ☐	No ☐

Please complete both sides of this document if you answered YES to any of the first series of questions (1–14).

Below is a list of problems that people sometimes have after experiencing a traumatic event. Please rate on a scale from 0–3 how much or how often these following things have occurred to you in the last two weeks:

0. Not at all
1. Once per week or less/ a little bit/ one in a while
2. 2 to 4 times per week/ somewhat/ half the time
3. 3 to 5 or more times per week/ very much/ almost always

1. Having upsetting thought or images about the traumatic event that come into your head when you did not want them to	0	1	2	3
2. Having bad dreams or nightmares about the traumatic event	0	1	2	3
3. Reliving the traumatic event (acting as if it were happening again)	0	1	2	3
4. Feeling emotionally upset when you are reminded of the traumatic event	0	1	2	3
5. Experiencing physical reactions when reminded of the traumatic event (sweating, increased heart rate)	0	1	2	3
6. Trying not to think or talk about the traumatic event	0	1	2	3
7. Trying to avoid activities or people that remind you of the traumatic event	0	1	2	3

APPENDIX F: PRESCREENING ASSESSMENT TOOL

8. Not being able to remember an important part of the traumatic event	0	1	2	3
9. Having much less interest or participating much less often in important activities	0	1	2	3
10. Feeling distant or cut off from the people around you	0	1	2	3
11. Feeling emotionally numb (unable to cry or have loving feelings)	0	1	2	3
12. Feeling as if your future hopes or plans will not come true	0	1	2	3
13. Having trouble falling or staying asleep	0	1	2	3
14. Feeling irritable or having fits of anger	0	1	2	3
15. Having trouble concentrating	0	1	2	3
16. Being overly alert	0	1	2	3
17. Being jumpy or easily startled	0	1	2	3

Glossary

Case study method: "An empirical inquiry that investigates a contemporary phenomenon (the 'case') in depth and within its real world context especially when boundaries between phenomenon and context may not be clearly evident."[1]

Classism: A form of structural oppression in which persons are discriminated against based on individual or group socio-economic status.[2]

Dehumanization: The denial of one's humanity.[3]

Domestication: The forceful implementation of the white master's and slavery's portrayal of black women as mammy; using black women to be responsible and care for the master's house, children and others, while denying black women the freedom to their life's course.[4]

Ethnography as pastoral care: An immersive research method in which one becomes a part of another's (individual or group) life experience in order to learn about and from them. It is also practiced as a form of pastoral listening, communal contextual and narrative model that acknowledges the weight of storytelling to get at ones human experience.[5]

Fractured Self: Among black women, the breaking of one's mental, emotional, and spiritual selves as a result of inhumane treatment, dehumanization, oppression, objectification (sexual and non-sexual), and domestication. This has led to a loss of freedom—freedom of voice, freedom

1. Yin, *Case Study Research*, 16.
2. Anderson et al., *Race, Class, Gender*, 61–67, 71–79.
3. Brooten et al., *Beyond Slavery*, 44–48.
4. McElya, *Clinging Mammy*, 160–61, 207–9.
5. Moschella, *Ethnography Pastoral Practice*, 4–5.

GLOSSARY

of interpretation, freedom to choose, freedom of personhood, and freedom to develop and become one's true self [6]—reframing of the term by this author specifically for black women.

Identity: This definition stems from Lee Butler, who asserts: "(1) Identity is formed in the context of relationship and is both intra-psychic and inter-psychic, and (2) identity is an expression of self-understanding. How one identifies oneself is the sum total of one's life experience."[7]

Lament: An expression of sorrow; mourning and wailing to express loss, pain, hurt, and suffering; the ability to cry out.[8]

Maafa: The genocide of Africans and their descendants during and after slavery.[9]

Midwifing: Is a method that facilitates empowerment, liberation, healing, and wholeness. The midwifing modality becomes a safe and sacred space that listens, holds, and cares for the thick narrative and multiple-reality experience shared within the therapeutic encounter. Empathy, listening, and patience are essential to this healthful approach, giving birth to opportunities for black women (and persons of color/marginalized) to move past merely surviving to thriving and becoming a cohesive self. New definition by the author.

Multigenerational transmission: An understanding of relational patterns that can be seen through relationships from generation to generation.[10]

Multiple-reality experience: Injurious experiences of slavery, domestication, dehumanization, racism, and classism that violate black women's mental, emotional, and physical health. This anguish was perpetrated on black women by white men, white women, and black men, and created a unique suffering experience—definition of new term by this author.

Oppression: My interpretation derives from my research and is formulated from a womanist framework, focusing on the exploitation and abuse of

---

6. Brooten et al., *Beyond Slavery*, 63–65.
7. Butler Jr., *Liberating Our Dignity*, 53.
8. McCrary, "Intimate Violence," 5–6.
9. Akinyela, "Wake Destruction," 250.
10. Nyengele, *African Women's Theology*, 133.

power asserted to the mind, body, and soul of persons. Oppression is any form of abuse that violates another's humanity.[11]

Racism: A form of prejudicial oppression that positions persons of one race as inferior and persons of another race as superior.[12]

Self: "Sense of being an independent center of initiative and perception, integrated with our most central ambitions and ideals and with our experience that our body and mind form a unit in space and a continuum in time."[13]

Sexism: A form of discrimination that oppresses a person based on gender.[14]

Slavery: My understanding of slavery is a compilation of my reading and research into the history and consequences of slavery in the Americas. In this research dissertation I refer to American slavery as an organized system that created vast economic wealth and privilege for whites, through selling of a commodity (Africans) and creating of product (children)—not just a simple system of ownership. Slavery stole the humanity of Africans and their descendants and instilled within their psyche a loss of freedom, humanity, and identity.[15]

Violence: Any violation against one's personhood; which includes physical, mental or emotional state that denies one's humanity and causes them harm. Hussein Abdilahi Bulhan defines violence as "any relation, process, or condition by which an individual or group violates the physical, social and/or psychological integrity of another person or group."[16]

Wholeness: From the researcher's interpretation, this would mean African-American women being able to deconstruct and integrate their multiple-reality reality experience, allowing them to be empowered to speak their truth and become whole in mind, body, and soul.[17]

---

11. Watkins Ali, *Survival Liberation*, 7.
12. Anderson et al., *Race, Class, Gender*, 61–71.
13. Kohut, *Restoration*, 177.
14. Anderson et al., *Race, Class, Gender*, 61–67, 80–82.
15. Brooten et al., *Beyond Slavery*, 1–18.
16. Bulhan, *Psychology Oppression*, 135.
17. McCrary, "Intimate Violence," 260–61.

Womanist: Originating in the writings of Alice Walker; a woman of color who is concerned with the well-being of her community, including men, women, and children. A womanist challenges all oppressive forces obstructing justice and is concerned with the struggle for survival of those deemed marginalized. This framework opposes all forms of oppression regardless of race, sex, class, sexuality, etc.[18]

18. Williams, *Sisters Wilderness*, 67.

Bibliography

Abbey-Lambertz, Kate. "These 15 Black Women Were Killed During Police Encounters, Their Lives Matter, Too." *Huffington Post*, February 13, 2015. www.huffingtonpost.com/2015/02/13/black-womens-lives-matter-police-shootings_n_6644276.html.

Akbar, Na'im. *Breaking the Chains of Psychological Slavery*. Tallahassee: Mind Productions and Associates, 1996.

Akinyela, M. "In the Wake of Destruction: Ujamaa Circle Process Therapy and Black Family Healing." In *Out of the Revolution: The Development of Africana Studies*, edited by Delores P. Aldridge and Carlene Young, 255–80. New York: Lexington, 2000.

Aldridge, Delores P., and Carlene Young, eds. *Out of the Revolution: The Development of Africana Studies*. Lanham, MD: Lexington, 2000.

Anderson, Margaret L., and Patricia Hill Collins, eds. *Race, Class, and Gender: An Anthology*. 6th ed. St. Louis: Chalice, 2006.

Anderson, Talmadge, and James Steward. *Introduction to African American Studies: Transdisciplinary Approaches and Implications*. Baltimore: Black Press Classics, 2007.

Belgrane, Faye Z., and Kevin W. Allison. *African American Psychology from Africa to America*. Thousand Oaks, CA: Sage, 2010.

Bell, E. J., and S. M. Nkoma. *Our Separate Ways: Black and White Women and the Struggle for Professional Identity*. Boston: Harvard Business School Press, 2001.

Berzoff, Joana, et al., eds. *Inside and Outside In: Psychodynamic Clinical Theory and Psychopathology in Contemporary Multicultural Context*. New York: Rowman & Littlefield, 2004.

Bidwell, Duane R., and Jorettta L. Marshall. *The Formation of Pastoral Counselors: Challenges and Opportunities*. Binghamton, NY: Hawthorne Pastoral, 2006.

Black Lives Matter. "Freedom & Justice for all Black Lives." https://blacklivesmatter.com.

Boyd-Franklin, Nancy. *Black Families in Therapy: Understanding the African American Experience*. 2nd ed. New York: Guildford, 2003.

Braxton, Brad R. "Lifting the Veil: The Shoah and the Maafa in Conversation." *Perspectives in Religious Studies* 38 (2011) 185–93.

Brooten, Bernadette J., and Jacqueline L. Hazelton, eds. *Beyond Slavery: Overcoming Its Religious and Sexual Legacies*. Black Religion, Womanist Thought, Social Justice. New York: Palgrave Macmillian, 2010.

Bulhan, Hussein Abdilahi. *Frantz Fanon and the Psychology of Oppression*. New York: Plenun, 1988.

———. *The Psychology of Oppression*. New York: Plenun, 1988.

Butler, Lee H. *Liberating Our Dignity and Saving Our Souls*. St. Louis: Chalice, 2006.

BIBLIOGRAPHY

Cannon, Katie G. *Black Womanist Ethics*. American Academy of Religion Academy Series 60. Atlanta: Scholars, 1988.

Cannon, Katie G., et al. *Womanist Theological Ethics: A Reader*. Louisville: Westminster John Knox, 2011.

Carillo, Ricardo, and Jerry Tello. *Family Violence and Men of Color: Healing the Wounded Male Spirit*. Focus on Men. New York: Springer, 2008.

Caruth, Cathy, ed. *Trauma: Explorations in Memory*. Baltimore: Johns Hopkins University Press, 1998.

Coleman, Monica A., ed. *Ain't I a Womanist, Too? Third-Wave Womanist Religious Thought*. Minneapolis: Fortress, 2013.

———. *Making a Way Out of No Way: A Womanist Theology*. Minneapolis: Fortress, 2008.

Collins, Patricia Hill. *Black Sexual Politics: African Americans, Gender, and the New Racism*. New York: Routledge, 2004.

Comas-Diaz, Lillian, and Beverly Greene, eds. *Women of Color: Integrating Ethnic and Gender Identities in Psychotherapy*. New York: Guildford, 1994.

Cone, James C., and Gayraud S. Wilmore, eds. *Black Theology: A Documentary History*. Vol. 2. Maryknoll, NY: Orbis, 2005.

Cooper, Tracey, and Tina Dame. "Women's Perceptions of a Midwife's Role: An Initial Investigation." *British Journal of Midwifery* 21 (2013) 264–72.

Cooper-White, Pamela. *Braided Selves: Collected Essays on Multiplicity, God, and Persons*. Eugene: Cascade Books, 2011.

———. *The Cry of Tamar: Violence against Women and the Church's Response*. Minneapolis: Fortress, 1995.

———. *Many Voices: Pastoral Psychotherapy in Relational and Theological Perspective*. Minneapolis: Fortress, 2007.

———. *Shared Wisdom: Use of the Self in Pastoral Care and Counseling*. Minneapolis: Fortress, 2004.

Crawford, A. Elaine Brown. *Hope in the Holler: A Womanist Theology*. Louisville: Westminster John Knox, 2002.

Crumpton, Stephanie A. *Crafting: A Womanist Pastoral Theological Exploration of African American Women and Self Recovery from Intimate Violence*. Decatur, GA: Columbia Theological Seminary, 2012.

———. *A Womanist Pastoral Theology against Intimate Violence and Cultural Violence*. Black Religion, Womanist Thought, Social Justice. New York: Palgrave Macmillan, 2014.

Donovan, Roxanne A. "To Blame or not to Blame: Influences of Target Race and Observer Sex on Rape Blame Attribution." *Journal of Interpersonal Violence* 22 (2007) 722–36.

Dyrness, William A., and Veli-Matti Karkkainen. *Global Dictionary of Theology: A Resource for the World Wide Church*. Downers Grove, IL: InterVarsity, 2008.

Edwards, Ashley N. "Dynamics of Economic Well-Being: Poverty, 2009–2011." United States Census Bureau Report, January 2014.

Fanon, Frantz. *The Wretched of the Earth*. New York: Grove, 2005.

Ford, David F., and Rachel Muers, eds. *An Introduction to Christian Theology since 1918: The Modern Theologians*. 3rd ed. Malden, MA: Blackwell, 2005.

Foster, Frances Smith. "Mammy's Daughters; Or the DNA of a Feminist Sexual Ethics." In *Beyond Slavery: Overcoming Its Religious and Sexual Legacies*, edited by Bernadette

BIBLIOGRAPHY

J. Brooten and Jacqueline L. Hazelton, 267–86. Black Religion, Womanist Thought, Social Justice. New York: Palgrave Macmillan, 2010.

Gaspar, David Barry, and Darlene Clark Hine, eds. *More than Chattel: Black Women and Slavery in the Americas*. Blacks in the Diaspora. Bloomington: Indiana University Press, 1996.

Geggus, David P. "Slave and Free Colored Women in St. Dominique." In *More Than Chattel: Black Women and Slavery in the Americas*, edited David Barry Gaspar and Darlene Clark Hine, 259–78. Blacks in the Diaspora. Bloomington: Indiana University Press, 1996.

Gillespie, Carmen, ed. *Toni Morrison: Forty Years in the Clearing*. Lanham, MD: Bucknell University Press, 2012.

Glave, Dianne D. *Rooted in the Earth: Reclaiming the African Environmental Heritage*. Chicago: Hill, 2010.

Grant, Brian W. *A Theology for Pastoral Psychotherapy: God's Play in Sacred Spaces*. New York: Haworth, 2001.

Greenberg, Jay R., and Stephen A. Mitchell. *Object Relations in Psychoanalytic Theory*. Boston: Harvard University Press, 1983.

Hayes, Diana L. "Feminist Theology, Womanist Theology: A Black Catholic Perspective." In *Black Theology: A Documentary History*, edited by James C. Cone and Gayraud S. Wilmore, 325–35. Vol. 2. Maryknoll, NY: Orbis, 2005.

Healey, Joseph F. *Race, Ethnicity, and Gender: Selected Readings*. Thousand Oak: Pine Forge, 2007.

Henderson, Mae G. *Speaking In Tongues and Dancing Diaspora: Black Women Writing, and Performing*. New York: Oxford University Press, 2014.

Hill, Markeva Gwendolyn. *Womanism against Socially-Constructed Matriarchal Images: A Theoretical Model toward a Therapeutic Goal*. Black Religion, Womanist Thought, Social Justice. New York: Palgrave Macmillan, 2012.

Hopkins, Dwight. "Enslaved Black Women: A Theology of Justice and Reparations." In *Beyond Slavery: Overcoming Its Religious and Sexual Legacies*, edited by Bernadette J. Brooten and Jacqueline L. Hazelton, 287–306. Black Religion, Womanist Thought, Social Justice. New York: Palgrave MacMillan, 2010.

Horney, Karen. *Self-Analysis*. New York: Norton, 1942.

Jackson, Leslie C., and Beverly Greene, eds. *Psychotherapy with African American Women: Innovations in Psychodynamic Perspective and Practice*. New York: Gilford, 2000.

Johnson, Allan G. *Privilege, Power, and Difference*. 2nd ed. New York: McGraw-Hill, 2006.

Jones, Charisse, and Kumea Shorter-Gooden. *Shifting the Double Lives of Black Women in America*. New York: HarperCollins, 2004.

Kaner, Angelica, and Ernst Prelinger. *The Craft of Psychodynamic Psychotherapy*. New York: Aronson, 2005.

Kaufman, Gershen. *The Psychology of Shame: Theory and Treatment of Shame-Based Syndromes*. 2nd ed. New York: Springer, 1989.

Kirk-Duggan, Cheryl. *Misbegotten Anguish: A Theology and Ethics of Violence*. St. Louis: Chalice, 2001.

Kohut, Heinz. *How Does Analysis Cure?* Chicago: University of Chicago Press, 1971.

———. *The Restoration of Self*. New York: International Universities Press, 1977.

Lartey, Emmanuel. *In Living Colour: An Intercultural Approach to Pastoral Care and Counseling*. 2nd ed. London: Kingsley, 2003.

Lee, Valerie. *Granny Midwives and Black Women Writers: Double-Dutched Readings*. New York: Routledge, 1996.
Levy-Hussen, Aida. "Trauma and the Historical Turn in Black Literary Discourse." In *The Psychic Hold of Slavery: Legacies in American Expressive Culture*, edited by Soyica Diggs Colbert, et al., 195–211. New Brunswick, NJ: Rutgers University Press, 2016.
Lim, Russell F. *Clinical Manual of Cultural Psychiatry*. 2nd ed. Arlington: American Psychiatric, 2015.
Mabunda, Mpho L. *Contemporary Black Biography: Profiles from the International Black Community*. Vol. 8. Ann Arbor: University of Michigan Press, 1994.
Mattis, Jacqueline. "Jesus Is Your Savior, Not Your Man: Candid Talk about the Church, Sexuality, and the Role They Play in Our Quest to Be Loved and Fulfilled." In *Black Woman Redefined: Dispelling Myths and Discovering Fulfillment in the Age of Michelle Obama*, edited by Sophia Nelson, 131–60. Dallas: Bella, 2013.
McCrary, Carolyn L. "Intimate Violence against Black Women and Internalized Shame: A Womanist Pastoral Counseling Perspective." *Journal of the ITC* 28 (2001) 159–75.
———. "Wholeness of Women." *Journal of the ITC* 25 (1998) 258–94.
McElya, Micki. *Clinging to Mammy: The Faithful Slave in Twentieth-Century America*. Boston: Harvard University Press, 2002.
McFadyen, Alistair I. *The Call to Personhood: A Christian Theology of the Individual in Social Relationships*. New York: Cambridge University Press, 1990.
McGuire, Danielle. *At the Dark End of the Street: Black Women, Rape and Resistance—A New History of the Civil Rights Movement from Rosa Parks to the Rise of Black Power*. New York: Knopf, 2010.
McWilliams, Nancy. *Psychoanalytic Psychotherapy: A Practitioner's Guide*. New York: Guilford, 2004.
Meek Mill. "Face Down." *Dreamchasers 2*. Maybach Music Group, 2012. CD.
Mitchell, Stephen A., and Margaret J. Black. *Freud and Beyond: A History of Modern Psychoanalytic Thought*. New York: Basic, 1995.
Mitchem, Stephanie Y. *Introducing Womanist Theology*. Maryknoll, NY: Orbis, 2002.
Moore, Darnell L. "Theorizing the "Black Body" as a Site of Trauma: Implications for Theologies of Embodiment." *Theology & Sexuality* 15 (2009) 175–88.
Morrison, Toni. *Beloved*. New York: Vintage, 2004.
———. *The Bluest Eye*. New York: Washington Square, 1970.
———. *Forty Years in the Clearing*. Edited by Carmen R. Gillespie. Lanham, MD: Bucknell University Press, 2012.
Moschella, Mary Clark. *Ethnography as a Pastoral Practice: An Introduction*. Cleveland: Pilgrim, 2008.
Myers, Linda James. *Understanding an Afrocentric World View: Introduction to an Optimal Psychology*. Dubuque, IA: Hunt, 1988.
Myers, Linda James, et al. "Recommendations for the Psychological Treatment of Persons of African Descent." In *Psychological Treatment of Ethnic Minority Populations*, edited by the Council of National Psychological Associations for the Advancement of Ethnic Minority Interests, 4–32. Washington, DC: Association of Black Psychologists, 2003.
Nelson, Sophia, ed. *Black Woman Redefined: Dispelling Myths and Discovering Fulfillment in the Age of Michelle Obama*. Dallas: Bella, 2013.
Neuger, Christie C. *Counseling Women: A Narrative Approach*. Minneapolis: Fortress, 2001.

BIBLIOGRAPHY

Nyengele, Mpyana Fulgence. *African Women's Theology, Gender Relations, and Family Systems*. American University Studies; Series VII, Theology and Religion 229. New York: Lang, 2004.

Northup, Solomon. *12 Years a Slave*. 1853. Reprint, New York: Atria, 2013.

Perry, Tyler. *For Colored Girls*. 2010. Video file. Santa Monica, CA: Lionsgate, 2010.

Peterson, Shani. "Images of Sexual Stereotypes in Rap Videos and the Health of African American Female Adolescents." *Journal of Women's Health* 16 (2007) 1157–64.

Pinn, Anthony B. *Moral Evil and Redemptive Suffering: A History of Theodicy in African American Religious Thought*. Gainesville: University Press of Florida, 2002.

Razak, Arisika. "Embodying Womansim." In *Ain't I a Womanist Too: Third-Wave Womanist Religious Thought*, edited by Monica A. Coleman, 217–27. Minneapolis: Fortress, 2013.

Ritchie, Beth E. *Arrested Justice: Black Women, Violence and Americas Prison Nation*. New York: New York University Press, 2012.

Roberts, Dorothy. "The Paradox of Silence and Display: Sexual Violation of Enslaved Women and Contemporary Female Sexuality." In *Beyond Slavery: Overcoming Its Religious and Sexual Legacies*, edited by Bernadette J. Brooten and Jacqueline L. Hazelton, 41–60. Black Religion, Womanist Thought, Social Justice. New York: Palgrave Macmillan, 2010.

Rodgers, Carolyn. "How I Got Ovah." In *Writing African American Women: K–Z*, edited by Elizabeth Ann Beaulieu, 177. Westport, CT: Greenwood, 2006.

Rutan, Scott J., et al. *Psychodynamic Group Psychotherapy*. 2nd ed. New York: Guilford, 1993.

Seeley, Karen M. *Cultural Psychotherapy: Working with Culture in the Clinical Encounter*. Lanham, MD: Aronson, 2006.

Shange, Ntozake. *For Colored Girls Who Have Considered Suicide/When the Rainbow Is Enuf*. New York: Scribner, 2010.

Sheppard, Phillis Isabella. *Self, Culture, and Others in Womanist Practical Theology*. Black Religion, Womanist Thought, Social Justice. New York: Palgrave Macmillan, 2011.

Smith, Archie, Jr. *The Relational Self: Ethics and Therapy from a Black Church Perspective*. Nashville: Abingdon, 1982.

Smith, Archie, Jr., and Ursula Riedel-Pfaefflin. *Siblings by Choice: Race, Gender, and Violence*. St. Louis: Chalice, 2004.

Smith, Margaret Charles, and Linda Janet Holmes. *Listen to Me Good: The Life Story of an Alabama Midwife*. Columbus: Ohio State University Press, 1996.

Smith, Merril D. *Encyclopedia of Rape*. Westport, CT: Greenwood, 2004.

Snorton, Teresa E. "The Legacy of the African American Matriarch: New Perspectives for Pastoral Care." In *Through the Eyes of Women: Insights for Pastoral Care*, edited by Jeannie Stevenson Moessner, 50–55. Minneapolis: Fortress, 1996.

Spielberg, Steven. *The Color Purple*. 1985. DVD. Burbank, CA: Warner Home Video, 2003.

Stevenson-Moessner, Jeanne, ed. *Through the Eyes of Women: Insights for Pastoral Care*. Minneapolis: Fortress, 1996.

Stevenson-Moessner, Jeanne, and Teresa Snorton. *Women Out of Order: Risking Change and Creating Care in a Multicultural World*. Minneapolis: Fortress, 2010.

Sung Park, Andrew. *From Hurt to Healing: A Theology of the Wounded*. Nashville: Abingdon, 2004.

Taft, Casey T., et al. "Intimate Partner Violence against African American Women: An Examination of the Socio-Cultural Context." *Aggression and Violent Behavior* 14 (2009) 50–58.

Thurman, Howard. *The Creative Encounter*. Richmond, IN: Friends United, 1972.

———. *Disciplines of the Spirit*. Richmond, IN: Friends United, 1963.

Townes, Emilie M. "From Mammy to Welfare Queen: Images of Black Women in Public Policy Formation." In *Beyond Slavery: Overcoming Its Religious and Sexual Legacies*, edited by Bernadette J. Brooten and Jacqueline L. Hazelton, 61–74. Black Religion, Womanist Thought, Social Justice. New York: Palgrave Macmillan, 2010.

———. *Womanist Ethics and the Cultural Production of Evil*. Black Religion, Womanist Thought, Social Justice. New York: Palgrave Macmillan, 2006.

Townsend, Cheryl. "The 'Loves' and 'Troubles' of African American Women's Bodies: The Womanist Challenge to Cultural Humiliation and Community Ambivalence." In *Womanist Theological Ethics: A Reader*, edited by Katie Cannon, et al. Louisville: Westminster John Knox, 2011.

Townsend, Loren. *Introduction to Pastoral Counseling*. Nashville: Abingdon, 2009.

Truth, Sojourner. "Women's Rights Convention Address, Akron Ohio, 1851." In *Encyclopedia of American Social Movements*, edited by Immanuel Ness, 57. Vol. 4. New York: Routledge, 2015.

Walker, Alice. *The Color Purple*. New York: Harcourt, 2003.

———. *In Search of Our Mothers' Gardens*. New York: Harcourt, 1983.

Walker-Barnes, Chanequa. *Too Heavy a Yoke: Black Women and the Burden of Strength*. Eugene: Cascade Books, 2014.

Wallace, Beverly R. "A Womanist Legacy of Trauma, Grief and Loss." In *Women Out of Order: Risking Change and Creating Care in a Multicultural World*, edited by Jeanne Stevenson-Moessner and Teresa Snorton, 43–56. Minneapolis: Fortress, 2010.

Watkins Ali, Carroll. *Survival and Liberation: Pastoral Theology in African American Context*. St. Louis: Chalice, 1999.

West, Traci C. *Wounds of the Spirit: Black Women, Violence, and Resistance Ethics*. New York: New York University Press, 1999.

White, Michael. *Maps of Narrative Practice*. New York: Norton, 2007.

Williams, Delores. *Sisters in the Wilderness: The Challenge of Womanist God-Talk*. Maryknoll, NY: Orbis, 1993.

Wimberly, Edward P. *African American Pastoral Care*. Revised ed. Nashville: Abingdon, 1991.

Woodard, James, and Stephen Pattison, eds. *The Blackwell Reader in Pastoral and Practical Theology*. Blackwell Readings in Modern Theology. Malden, MA: Blackwell, 2000.

Wriggins, Jennifer. "Rape, Racism, and the Law." In *Race, Class, and Gender: An Anthology*, edited by Margaret L. Andersen and Patricia Hill Collins, 424–31. 9th ed. United States: Cengage Learning, 2015.

Yin, Robert K. *Case Study Research: Design and Methods*. Thousand Oaks, CA: Sage, 2014.

www.ingramcontent.com/pod-product-compliance
Lightning Source LLC
Chambersburg PA
CBHW071456150426
43191CB00008B/1368